How to Coach Speed Technique

by

Phil Campbell, M.S., M.A., FACHE-R, ACSM - CPT

2020

www.40speed.com
www.speed-science.com
email: info@40speed.com
ISBN-13: 978-0-578-52638-6
Library of Congress Control Number: 2019907632

This book is designed to provide information in regard to the subject matter covered for healthy athletes. This book is sold with the understanding that the publisher, author and advisors are not rendering medical advice or any other professional services. An examination by a physician needs to be performed BEFORE attempting sprint exercise discussed in this book, or any fitness, flexibility or strength training program. Sprinting is anaerobic exercise, the most demanding form of exercise, and it has the most risks.

The purpose of this book is to educate, expand thinking about speed training and athletic performance improvement as an information source for readers, and it is not medical advice, nor has it been evaluated by the FDA. The publisher, author, and advisors shall have neither liability nor responsibility to any person or entity with respect to any loss or damage caused or alleged to be caused directly or indirectly by the information and programs contained in this book. If you do not agree with the above, you may return to the publisher for a full refund.

2019 Printed in USA. Pollock Printing, 928 6th Ave S, Nashville, TN 37203
Graphics by Manoj Bhargav (https://manojbhargavindia.blogspot.com/
Photographs by the author unless otherwise stated
40speed.com
651 Paris Street
McKenzie, Tennessee 38201

Library of Congress Control Number: 2019907632
Cataloging-in-Publication
    Campbell, Phillip K.
    How to Coach Speed Technique
    Includes bibliographical references and index
    ISBN-13: 978-0-578-52638-6

1. Speed Technique 2. Speed Training 3. Coaching 4. Coaching Sports
4. Physical fitness 5. Strength & Conditioning 6. Sprint-Intensity
Training (SIT) 7. High-Intensity Interval Training (HIIT)

Contents

Part One *Ready*

Part Two *Set*

Part Three *GO!*

Ray Lewis III perfecting speed technique at the Under Armour Global HQ Performance Center powered by FX Fitness in Baltimore, Maryland

Working with Jerry Rice Jr. on speed technique at the Riekes Center in Menlo Park, California
www.Riekes.org

1

Speed Technique

The most important question I ask athletes flying in for two days of speed technique training is, "Do you remember the day you first learned how to run?"

Athletes typically look puzzled and respond, "No, am I supposed to?" This gets their attention and sets the stage for teaching speed technique.

Almost no one remembers the day they first learned how to run. We were so young, we don't remember it, and we weren't strong enough to position our bodies like trained sprinters. We started out running like cross-country runners, tall and upright, which is great technique for distance runners, but very poor technique for athletes in sprinting sports.

Most athletes, as well as most runners, run tall and upright. This is advantageous for endurance athletes because this type of running is propelled by type 1 slow-twitch muscle fiber and the heart muscle and the lungs don't have to work as hard as when sprinting fast. When the body moves efficiently propelled by slow fiber, runners can endure and run for long distances. They just aren't going to get there fast.

When untrained runners sprint, they remain tall and upright and move their legs and arms as fast as possible. This is also how most athletes position their bodies to sprint naturally, and they aren't living up to their speed potential until they become speed technique trained.

Speed technique training is simply teaching athletes how to position the body to force the recruitment of all three muscle-fiber types to propel linear, lateral and sports-specific, functional, sprint-running movements.

Speed Means Success in Many Sports

A great many sports are sprinting sports. Obviously, sprinting events in track & field would be sprinting sports. Football, soccer, rugby, lacrosse, softball, baseball and basketball are also sprint running sports.

Typically speaking, athletes can become successful at these sports learning and practicing the movements of their sport, if they can sprint 20 yards fast.

Starting from a backpedal, lateral stance or from a change-of-direction movement, if athletes can cover 20 yards fast, they will have a better opportunity to be successful in their sport.

If you are a sprint swimmer, this book may help you get from the dressing room to the pool faster, but you need a swim technique coach. Applying the training principles in this book will help build fast-muscle fiber on dry land and this will increase the number of endurance-producing mitochondria that transfer to the pool -- if, if, if -- if you have been trained in optimal stroke technique and practice optimal technique at race pace and faster.

Become a Speed Coach to You

This book gives coaches speed techniques so they can teach optimal speed mechanics to the athletes they coach. Speed technique training is a great fast-muscle fiber workout, but speed technique training IS NOT about the workout.

Speed technique training is much different than what most people think, and it's different than what is practiced in many athletic performance centers.

Of the 18,000 athletes I've worked with during the last 40 years, they come to me because they aren't living up to their speed potential.

Most athletes traveling to me for my two-session speed technique course are already enrolled in performance center training. While their physiques are improving, they are not significantly improving in speed because they don't know and practice optimal speed technique during training.

What most athletes are doing to get faster is a conditioning boot camp based on the premise that ground-based functional training will magically help athletes improve speed if they gain muscle and drop body fat.

This is a flawed concept contrary to new research discoveries about muscle fiber recruitment and the science of neuroplasticity, which teaches us how the brain, nervous system and muscle interact to recruit different muscle-fiber types to propel athletic movements. Sadly, this antiquated type of performance training reinforces and practices poor speed technique over-and-over again.

Speed technique training is more about the brain nervous system connection and how the brain sends messages to recruit more fast-muscle fiber to propel athletic movements.

Speed technique training is also about teaching athletes to become speed coaches to themselves so they can make corrections about body positioning during training and practice. When athletes practice faster, they recruit more fast fiber and they continue to get stronger and faster.

Your Body Adapts to the Way You Train

The number one principle in exercise science every expert seems to agree is the body adapts in a positive way to the way it's trained, (Selye, Hans (1950) *Stress and the General Adaptation Syndrome.* Jun 17; *British Medical Journal* (4667): 1383–1392. PMCID: PMC2038162. PMID: 15426759).

Adaptation to training simply means that if you want to run fast, you need to train fast. If an athlete, for example, trains heavy and slow, the body builds slow-twitch muscle fiber and the slow muscle cells get bigger and stronger. Fast-muscle fibers don't get stronger because they aren't being recruited during the slower movement work.

Training fast with intensity creates micro-trauma in the muscles propelling the movements. This starts the process that builds muscle. In essence, when we lift weights, we are intentionally trying to injure muscle fiber. Not pull or tear it. But at the cellular level, when we lift weights for example, the gains come after recovery. We don't leave the gym stronger after lifting. We are weaker after lifting.

During sleep, muscles heal and repair and they get larger and stronger. People say muscle has memory, but this statement can be misleading.

Muscle is a slave to the master. The master is the brain and the nervous system that connects to every muscle fiber in the body.

Speed technique training is targeting this system; brain to nervous system to force the recruitment of all three muscle-fiber types that propel specific sets of athletic movements.

Speed training is somewhat like driving down the freeway 70 MPH and pulling off to refuel. As you slow down to 50 MPH, you feel like it's only 20 MPH. Why? Your brain, nervous system and inner ear are acclimated to 70 MPH. When you slow down to 50 MPH after driving 70 MPH, it seems slow.

This same experience applies to athletes during practice. The body adapts to the way it's trained. Slow practice trains the brain and the nervous system to perform sluggish and much slower than potential. I can't tell you how many athletes have come to me thinking if they trained longer and ran more, this would help improve their speed. To the contrary, they are practicing to run slow over and over and over.

Speed Technique Coaching Process

Day One starts with linear speed technique after the General Warm-up and the Specific Warm-up, (which includes the three speed technique drills). Linear speed technique is the fundamental base other skills are built upon.

Lateral speed technique follows. Once linear speed technique is mastered and athletes have timed for 4 to 8 reps of 20-yard sprints focusing on one technique per rep, the lateral start is added. Next, the functional, position-specific speed technique work begins during the first two-hour session.

Day Two of speed technique training (called Speed Technique 102) is a repeat of the first day without the initial teaching time. We refine on the second day, and quickly get to *position-specific speed technique application* so athletes will take to the field what they learn during the two days of technique training.

This system teaches optimal mechanics for instant speed improvement that typically yields a two-tenths gain in the 20-yard sprint on the first day. This means the distance it took athletes to cover 15 to 16 yards before technique training, now, in the same amount of time, athletes cover 20 yards.

Meet Your Enemy, the *Exercise Paradox*

It is mission critical that athletes learn about the *athletic exercise paradox*. If you have read my articles or attended one of my Sprint 8 presentations during the last 30 years, you have heard me refer to the concepts behind the *exercise paradox* many times. The *exercise paradox* means the brain has an attraction for sedentary behaviors, (Cheval, B. (2018), *Avoiding sedentary behaviors requires more cortical resources than avoiding physical activity: An EEG study.* October. *Neuropsychologia* Volume 119, Pages 68-80).

The *athletic exercise paradox* explains why athletes subconsciously put the brakes on speed and never realize the brakes are on until they go through the speed technique learning process.

Your brain wants you to move with slow-muscle fiber propelling the movement in the endurance energy system so you can endure all day. In many respects *the brain thinks it's doing you a favor not to recruit fast-muscle fiber* to make every human movement easier. Your brain wants you to conserve the fast fiber in case you need it later for an emergency situation.

Energy for practice and playing sports comes from the amount of ATP-producing mitochondria in the muscle cells. The father of High Intensity Interval Training, Dr. Gary A. Dudley demonstrated back in 1982 that high-intensity cardio at near max intensity will multiply the number of energy-producing mitochondria in the muscle cells, which is the key for increasing energy levels and endurance in humans.

Here's the problem; the brain puts on brakes via the *exercise paradox* and the brakes stay on until you know how to release them and move forward.

I can't emphasize the importance of understanding the impact of the *athletic exercise paradox*. When coaches and parents watch speed technique training, it's easy to observe the body's natural default position for human movement. The body always performs human movement the easiest way possible by recruiting less muscle fiber in the endurance energy system.

Speed technique training is simply teaching athletes to do just the opposite of the natural default position. Rather than staying in slow-twitch, endurance mode, athletes learn how to position their bodies to force the recruitment of every muscle fiber possible to propel full-speed athletic movements.

Muscle Fiber Recruitment Science

When coaches and athletes understand the impact of the *exercise paradox* and how to overcome it, speed technique skills can be applied to make every athletic movement faster.

Muscle-fiber recruitment science now comes into play. Humans move in the default position propelled by slow-muscle fiber in the endurance energy system. The brain always sends the smaller slow-muscle fiber to accomplish a task first before the fast-muscle fiber is recruited. This is called *Henneman's Size Principle* and it has been tested several times over the years and proven to be reliable, (Henneman, E., Somjen, G. & Carpenter, D. (1965). *Functional significance of cell size in spinal motor neurons. Journal of Neurophysiology* 28, 560-580).

Specifically, the brain recruits the smallest muscle fiber (slow-twitch type I) first. When the brain senses the need to move faster, it recruits the fast-twitch IIa fiber (that moves 5 times faster than the slow) to accomplish the task. Using this fiber may make the team, but the athlete may still be on the bench. Recruiting super-fast IIx fiber wins games, get scholarships and lands large contracts.

When the brain senses the slow type I fiber and the fast IIa fiber aren't enough to get the job done, the brain and the nervous system recruits the IIx super-fast muscle fiber. This is the fast-twitch IIx fiber that moves 10 times faster than the slow, and the IIx fiber is what athletes need to strengthen to get faster, along with reprogramming the brain on how to move with optimal speed technique.

When all three muscle-fiber types are recruited, the heart muscle has to work a lot harder attempting to oxygenate quite literally twice the muscle fiber. When athletes train like this, they condition the anaerobic system, which is the type of conditioning needed for most sprinting-type sports.

This is why High-Intensity Interval Training (HIIT) started out with max-intensity exercise that forced the recruitment of all three muscle-fiber types. It gets superior results. But over the years, HIIT has become so watered down that I've had to start calling the *Sprint 8 Cardio Protocol* from my first two books by the title of *sprint cardio* rather than HIIT so people will understand the difference. And there is a huge difference in effort and results.

The current interpretation of HIIT is at best moderate-intensity exercise. HIIT today is hard, slow-fiber cardio, but it doesn't recruit super-fast fiber and this means the anaerobic process needed for most sports doesn't get conditioned.

Teaching athletes why it's necessary to recruit all three muscle-fiber types during practice and condition both processes of the heart muscle are mission critical in significantly improving energy levels necessary for sprinting sports.

I've only worked with two college soccer teams. Both won their respective national championships the year I worked with them. Most coaches think soccer is an endurance sport. Soccer is a repeated sprint sport requiring anaerobic conditioning and its by-product, aerobic conditioning. When soccer athletes train fast for repeated short sprints specific to their position, the whole team gets faster. Generally, a team can cover 20 yards in the same time they covered 15 yards by applying optimal technique they learn in two speed-technique sessions.

The reason why, this type of hard and fast training improves energy because it changes the body at the cellular level by multiplying the number of mitochondria in the muscle cells. Martin Gabala and Kirsten Burgomaster's research at the Department of Medicine, McMaster University in Canada shows you can double endurance capacity in three workouts per week in two weeks' time, (Bugormaster, K, Gabala, M. (2005) *Six sessions of sprint interval training increases muscle oxidative potential and cycle endurance capacity in humans J Appl Physiol* 98:1985-1990, doi:10.1152 / japplphysiol.01095.2004).

When recruiting all three muscle-fiber types, this conditions the anaerobic process as well as the aerobic process of the heart muscle. Researchers report:

*Sprint Interval Training (SIT) improves aerobic capacity in healthy, young people. Relative to continuous endurance training of moderate intensity, SIT presents an equally **effective alternative with a reduced volume of activity,*** (Gist, N. (2014 Feb), *Sprint interval training effects on aerobic capacity: a systematic review and meta-analysis. Sports Med. 44(2):269-79).*

When athletes try to sprint faster, their bodies go back to the *default* position similar to the way we learned how to run -- tall and upright with arms too close to the chest. Athletes will remain in *default* until they learn optimal speed technique, and consistently practice fast to recruit and strengthen all three muscle-fiber types propelling position-specific movements. Anaerobic conditioning, needed for many sports, is the positive by-product of speed training.

Bottom line, the solution for overcoming the *exercise paradox* is for athletes to understand muscle-fiber recruitment science and discovering the best way to apply optimal speed technique for every athletic movement they perform.

Recruiting IIX Fast-Fiber Motor Units

When teaching athletes how to recruit fast-twitch muscle fiber, it is helpful to explain how the super-fast IIx muscle fiber is significantly larger and stronger than the slow-twitch fiber. The super-fast fiber also has many more muscle fibers assembled in its motor units.

This process begins with the brain sending messages down the spinal cord where they are ultimately connected to every skeleton muscle in the body to make muscle move. Muscle-fiber types receive instruction from the brain in groups called *motor units.* The nerves that connect from the spinal cord to muscle are called *motor nerves* or motor neurons.

While muscle-fiber types are independent components of muscle, they are recruited in groups of the same fiber type. When we speak of muscle recruitment, this really means type I motor units, type IIa fast fiber motor units, and type IIx motor units. They are being recruited in groups inside the same muscle by their type.

The following graphic shows muscle fiber recruitment for the three different motor units inside the same muscle. Slow type I motor unit, shown on the left, is composed of the small type I fibers, and it is recruited for general movement. Slow muscle fibers are dark red because they get more blood supply. And very important, they are the smallest fibers connected to their motor nerves. Because these fibers are small and there aren't a lot of these, the heart muscle doesn't have to work hard to oxygenate a few slow-twitch muscle cells in a motor unit. You can endure longer only using this muscle fiber to propel movement, but you won't get there fast.

The two fast fiber motor units, IIa and IIx, lay dormant allowing the slow fiber motor units to do all the work. Not getting used means the fast fiber doesn't get strong and athletes don't get faster. When hard and fast movements demand the strength and contraction speed of more muscle, the large fast-twitch IIa motor units are recruited next. Needing even more muscle to accomplish a speed burst, the extra-large type IIx units are recruited last.

Notice in the graphic the size difference of the super-fast fibers and how many more fibers are in the IIx motor unit. Slow type I motor units may have 10 to 180 fibers that all move simultaneously when contracted.

Fast IIa and super-fast IIx motor units may have 300 to 800 fast-twitch fibers in a motor unit, (Costill, Wilmore J (1994) *Physiology of Sport and Exercise.* Human Kinetics, p 36). This explains why track sprinters can't sprint full speed for very long. For a 100-meter sprint, the fast fiber last for 10 to 12 seconds. For 200 meters, 20 to 23 seconds and the fast IIx fiber inside of the IIx motor units are totally exhausted.

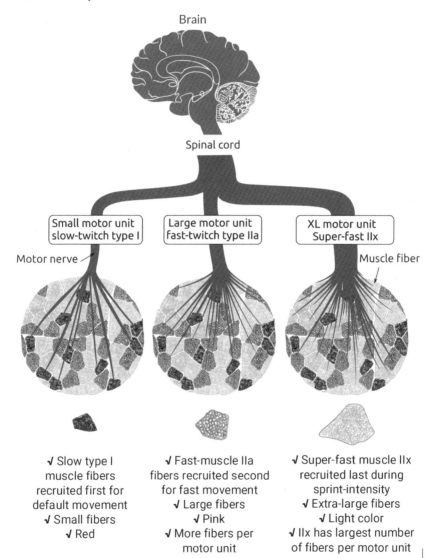

Brain

Spinal cord

Small motor unit
slow-twitch type I

Large motor unit
fast-twitch type IIa

XL motor unit
Super-fast IIx

Motor nerve

Muscle fiber

√ Slow type I
muscle fibers
recruited first for
default movement
√ Small fibers
√ Red

√ Fast-muscle IIa
fibers recruited second
for fast movement
√ Large fibers
√ Pink
√ More fibers per
motor unit

√ Super-fast muscle IIx
recruited last during
sprint-intensity
√ Extra-large fibers
√ Light color
√ IIx has largest number
of fibers per motor unit

Graphics by Manoj Bhargav
manojbhargavindia.blogspot.com

When all three motor units are recruited inside a strand of muscle (shown below), the heart muscle has to work at near-maximum intensity as it attempts to oxygenate significantly more muscle fibers that are substantially larger than the dark slow type I fibers.

Using this graphic by Manoj Bhargav is helpful for teaching athletes muscle recruitment science.

Muscle Fiber Types

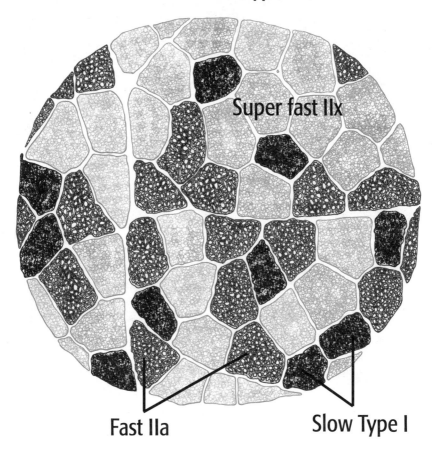

Bottom line, your body is a temple, and you have to treat it that way. That's how God designed it. - Ray Lewis

Teaching muscle fiber recruitment after warm-up and before the speed technique drills to Ray Lewis III, Ralin Lewis & Rahsaan Lewis, sons of NFL Hall of Fame member Ray Lewis who looks on with coach Doug Lawson, LaRian Finney (www.legendsaccess.com) and his son Rian at the Under Armour Global HQ Performance Center powered by Fitness FX in Baltimore

Speed Gives Athletes Healthy Swagger

Everyone who has played sports, especially basketball, knows *confidence* (frequently referred to as swag and swagger) helps athletes and teams perform better. Sometimes swagger helps teams perform better than expected.

Athletes and teams with low confidence levels don't take risks. They over focus on security. They go for fake moves. They react slower. They play *not to lose*. At end of the game, athletes with low-confidence levels typically perform below their potential.

Athletes and teams with swagger take calculated risks and play to win. At the end of the game, they seemingly performed better than their potential.

Confidence makes game-winning tackles. Confidence makes consistently solid plays the entire game. Confidence makes big plays when the pressure is turned up to the highest level, and it makes buzzer-beater winning shots.

Observing the greatest clutch basketball athlete of all time, Michael Jordan, makes a strong case for superior speed being the main source of confidence. When an athlete like Jordan knows he is faster than his opponent, he has confidence and wants the ball in his hands for the last shot.

At the end of a tie game with the national championship on the line, Michael Jordan wanted the ball. He wanted the ball because he was confident he could use his speed to get an open shot. How did he know that? He discovered he was faster than his opponent during the game.

You may have heard a coach say post game, *once our team got settled in and got their confidence, we played much bette*r. This means it took a little time in the game before the athletes realized they could match or exceed their opponent's speed.

When coaching a speed technique camp at Calallen High School in Corpus Christi Texas a few years ago, the head football coach Phil Danaher, who on his 427th win became the coach with the most wins in Texas High School football history, told me something I will never forget; *I know my players are getting faster. I can physically see them run faster the first day. But even if they didn't, they believe they are faster and this will make them practice fast and put extra effort in trying to make a play.*

I learned a lot about the impact of speed technique training from this wise coach with a record that proves he knows how to coach and win games.

Speed is confidence. In many cases, the source of confidence is knowing the athlete and your team has superior speed. Speed is confidence in sprint running sports like football, soccer, lacrosse, rugby, basketball, hockey, and for many positions in baseball and softball.

Michael Jordan set the standard high in many areas of athletic performance. Back in the day when strength training was thought to potentially mess with a basketball player's shot, Jordan performed strength training before games to get his body in work mode. His superior speed and the pump from strength training clearly contributed to his enhanced confidence on the court.

When athletes know they are faster than the competition, this gives them confidence, and swagger makes big plays to win games.

Observe Mike Tyson. Talking about an athlete with swag. He had it. Why? When you watch his film, it's clear. He was faster than his competition.

Mike Tyson is known for his power. Power is largely dependent on velocity of movement. Hitting an opponent hard and slow doesn't do a lot of damage. Hard and fast does.

Observe Muhammad Ali. He brought swag to a whole new level in athletic performance. Watch his film and you'll see why he was so confident. Speed. Ali was faster than his opponents.

Speed is the source of confidence.

A coach may try the strategy of having football athletes not shake hands with their opponents during the coin toss and teach some horrible things to their athletes in an attempt to give them swagger. This is not a good decision. The best way to give athletes and your team confidence is speed technique training.

Teach and practice speed technique based on the principles in this book, and you'll build healthy athletic confidence. The shake hands refusal strategy doesn't work, and frankly, coaches using this method should be terminated because it teaches the exact opposite of what sports are intended to do -- character building, working with others successfully in a group setting, goal setting and achievement within the rules of the game, while developing the healthy motivation to exercise for a lifetime.

Speed technique training does a lot more than just making athletes faster. It gives them confidence.

Improve Speed with Neuroplasticity

Neuroplasticity simply means the brain is like plastic. It changes with practice to help humans move faster and more efficiently.

When we learn new optimal speed techniques and practice optimal techniques full speed to improve athletic performance, we are actually applying the science of neuroplasticity, which is the KEY to improving speed and quickness for athletic movements.

The full definition of neuroplasticity is *the human brain adapts to changing demands by altering its functional and structural properties, which results in learning and acquiring skills*, (Budde, H. (2016) *Neuroscience of Exercise: Neuroplasticity and Its Behavioral Consequence,* Neural Plasticity. Article ID 3643879, http://dx.doi.org/10.1155/2016/3643879).

When we learn anything new, like a new cell phone or a faster way of performing an athletic movement, the brain has an interesting and important response. The brain remodels itself according to the way it's used. It adapts to the way it's trained just like our muscles, tendons and ligaments do when we perform speed and strength training.

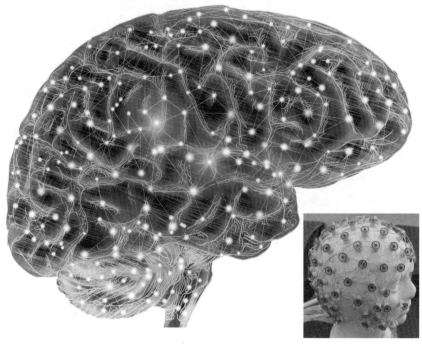

In learning mode, EEG cap measurement shows the human brain lights up as it seeks to find the best pathways to accomplish the task

When we get a new smart phone, for example, the simple tasks of turning it on and off and finding apps are initially slow because we don't know the phone yet. If we were wearing an EEG cap to measure the brain's response to new phone movement, the whole brain would light up as being used. The whole brain lights up hunting for the best neural pathways to accomplish the task.

As we use the phone over-and-over and the brain practices smart phone movements, the whole brain stops lighting up and only the pathways needed to execute the movements light up. The brain has learned and remodeled itself so it only uses the needed pathways to execute new smart phone maneuvers.

Six months later, the brain continues to remodel like warm plastic and we make cell phone movements extremely fast while on autopilot, almost without thinking about it. And the movements have become very fast.

When your fingers are flying around your phone getting things done, some people may describe this as *being in the zone*, which is similar to how we may describe an athlete who has superior focus to accomplish the task no matter what obstacles appear.

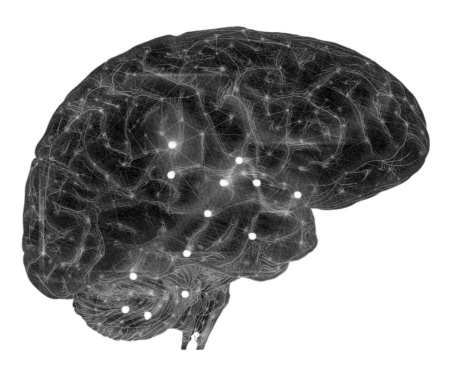

Performing a proficient skill, EEG shows the brain has eliminated unnecessary pathways making movement faster

The same process happens when learning a new video game. Male athletes seem to relate to the video game analogy.

Learning a new video game is slow at first. As the brain remodels learning and applying new video game skills, those specific movements become faster and faster as the unneeded pathways are eliminated.

This is what speed technique training is all about. It is essentially learning how to best play the speed technique video game in the brain so it knows how to position the body optimally to force recruitment of all three muscle-fiber types that move the human body faster.

Sounds simple I know, but this is where Malcolm Galdwell's *10,000-Hour Rule* from his book *Outliers: The Story of Success* comes into play. His book deals with exceptionally successful people who operate at the extreme outer edge of what is statistically possible. His point is, it takes 10 years and 10,000 reps to become an expert at a skill whether it's music, hockey or building a company like Microsoft.

While it doesn't take 10 years to get faster, it does take practicing optimal speed technique three days a week after learning Speed Technique 101 and 102 to keep getting faster and faster. With practicing optimal speed technique, improvement continues both in the brain through neuroplasticity and through the recruitment of all three muscle-fiber types so athletes keep getting stronger and stronger.

Every time athletes practice optimal speed technique at 100% full speed, great things happen in the brain and in the muscle fibers. What happens when athletes practice at 80% speed? This is a no brainer. Practicing at 80% speed is essentially practicing to perform slow. While it's fine to learn new football plays slower than full speed, until those plays are practiced several times full speed, the brain will not allow athletes perform up to their potential.

Recommended

Spark: The Revolutionary New Science of Exercise
by John J. Ratey, MD

The Quest for the Perfect Athlete
Documentary film by Benoit Laborde

2

Speed Training Warm-up

There are many different ways to warm-up athletes. Some methods take too long and rob valuable time for more productive work. The warm-up for speed training can take longer than other forms of training depending on the environment. Coaches should consistently assess athletes and adapt to the ambient conditions.

There are two parts to a speed warm-up, *general warm-up* and *specific warm-up*. The goal of the *general warm-up* is to raise the body temperature one degree and increase blood flow through muscles to help prevent injury and get muscles, joints, tendons, and ligaments in work mode.

The *specific warm-up* takes it a step further by preparing the body's highest level of intensity, full speed, all-out sprint running.

If it's cold outside, there may need to be some extra general warm-up reps based on assessment. Hot temperatures outside where athletes risk dehydration before practice is over will need an adequate, but minimalistic warm-up since they are starting out with elevated temperature already. This environment may need less reps or a walk back to start *extra recovery* between reps to ensure the body is in work mode and ready for the highest intensity level of exercise, fast-fiber recruiting speed training.

The speed technique drills in the following chapter are also part of the warm-up process. The speed technique drills help athletes play the speed video game in the brain to rehearse optimal speed technique, broken down into three parts.

The goal of the coach is to accomplish an *adequate* warm-up that is somewhat minimalistic so athletes have more energy for the hard and fast sprints during the workout.

Warm-up reps are dynamic plyometric drills that end with a 5-yard sprint out, initially at 50% speed and focusing on good technique with arms and body lean. Over the years, I've learned the *exercise paradox* kicks in even during the warm-up, and I counter it in advance by explaining to athletes; *50% speed is actually 100% full speed, minus 50% -- and it's faster than most think.*

In a perfect world, Rep #1 would be 10-15 yards of the drill and end with a 50% speed 5-yard sprint out (followed by a 5 to 10-yard slow down).

Rep #2 is a 10-15 yard drill with a 60% speed sprint out.

Rep #3 is a 10-15 yard drill with a 70% speed sprint out.

The 5-yard sprint out gets progressively faster every rep. The sprint out multitasks warm-up with the opportunity for coaches to begin checking technique application. Should coaches see athletes sprint out high and upright with arms too tight to their chests, this is poor speed technique. Sloppy technique during the sprint out (after the first few reps) means athletes are rehearsing poor technique. It means I haven't given you the tools necessary to teach athletes why it's mission-critical important to practice optimal speed technique even during warm-up sprint outs.

It is difficult to use the correct forward-body lean and speed-arm mechanics when moving at 50% speed. However, when athletes get to the faster 5-yard sprint outs, (other than the first day during Speed Technique 101), athletes should be beginning to apply speed technique of how to position the body to recruit more fast fiber to propel the sprint out.

When coaches see athletes applying speed technique consistently in practice and during the warm-up sprint outs, then they know their athletes have learned the techniques and they are beginning to apply them consistently. This is very positive because it means the new techniques are on the way to becoming internalized speed skill.

General Warm-up

Goal: Accomplish an adequate general warm-up in minimal time conserving energy for full-speed intensity work

1. Side slides

10-15 yard drill with 5-yard sprint out

Athletes do 3 lateral slides, a moving flip hip switch to face the other side, continuing the 3 slides, switching every 3 slides for 10 to 15 yards, finish with the 5-yard (50% speed) sprint out.

2. A-Skips

10-15 yard drill with 5-yard sprint out at 60% speed

Coaching cue: Skipping with knees coming up to waist (belt) level. Hands should be moving from back-pocket to chin level and away from the chest.

3. High knees

10-15 yards with 5-yard sprint out at 80% speed

Coaching cue: Full-speed drill, hard and fast. Knees waist level. The speed sprint out (at 80% speed) is where coaches should look for the beginning of a positive forward lean with animated arm technique.

4. Butt kickers

10-15 yard drill
with 5-yard sprint out
at 80 to 90% speed.
Knees pointed to the ground.

5. Karaoke left and right

15 - 20 yards no sprint out

Unlike a Linebacker Karaoke, the Speed Karaoke is a high, waist level knee over movement, hard and fast, and the back leg movement is passive and soft. The most important part of this drill is the HIP FLIP from front to back. Coaching cue: Knee up and over is waist level. Hip flip where hips are facing forward then flipping to facing back. This is not a slight change-of-direction for the hips. Coaches should look for a dramatic HIP FLIP where hips face forward to back during the drill as shown below.

6. Tapioca left and right

10 yards no sprint out

Tapioca is called many different things, Fast Feet, Fire Feet. It's like the Karaoke drill, but feet stay close to the ground and it resembles full-speed salsa dancing with quick HIP FLIP movements. Like Karaoke, it's more about the quick HIP FLIP movements.

7. Backward reach run

15 -20 yards no sprint out

The goal is backward running with a high back leg, near jumping / bounding step. Unlike a defensive back backpedal, athletes should be facing backward at the start line with upper body bent forward from the waist. Coaching cue: Reach with the back leg waist level high for 15 yards. No sprint out.

8. Water

Quick fluid break. Next is the specific warm-up multi-tasked with the three mission-critical speed technique drills.

*A coach should not only **tell** athletes what is expected, but also **clarify why** it is expected, and how it will benefit them personally.*

- Vince McConnell

McConnellAthletics.com

3

Speed Technique Drills

Three speed-technique drills teach and rehearse perfect movements for optimal body positioning and sprint mechanics broken down into three parts. The drills also serve to complete the *specific warm-up* to prepare the body to move faster than ever before.

The three drills are *leg drives* to teach *drive phase* acceleration technique, *claw drill* to teach *fly phase* technique, and *pocket-chin arms* (frequently called *butt bumpers*) to teach optimal-arm mechanics for both *drive phase* and *fly phase*.

I can't over-emphasize the importance of these three drills. We are breaking down optimal speed technique into three parts. Master these three parts and train your athletes to know and feel optimal speed technique. It does take focused work to get faster while sprinting full speed focusing on all three technical components. This will not happen until athletes learn to feel optimal technique.

Once athletes master the three drills during the first workout or two, these drills become rehearsal of the major components of speed, multi-tasked with the *specific warm-up*. These drills also prepare the brain and the body to move faster than ever before.

Drive Phase vs. Fly Phase

Two important definitions your athletes need to understand. These terms will be used throughout this book, *drive phase* and *fly phase.* The positioning of the body is completely different in *drive phase* and *fly phase* sprint running.

The rules also are different for *fly phase* and *drive phase. Fly phase* is upright running. As discussed in Chapter 1, the way we first learned how to run is grossly incorrect sprinting technique for short, quick acceleration bursts of speed. We initially learned how to run when we were small and much weaker and incapable of placing the body in the optimal sprinting position.

Drive phase is starting from a dead start and sprinting up to 20 yards. While *drive phase* length can slightly vary from athlete to athlete by 5 to 10 yards, for teaching purposes, we will use 0 to 20 yards for *drive phase* discussions.

The starting position in *drive phase* can be a two-hands down sprinters track start. It can be a 3-point football combine start, or a soccer back pedal to an abrupt change-of-direction forward sprint to the ball. It could be a softball / baseball athlete releasing the bat and sprinting to beat the throw to first.

Drive phase begins anytime an athlete starts sprinting as fast as possible from a dead still position, or the start is from a change-of-direction move where it takes all the power the body can produce to accelerate the body's mass from slow to full speed.

Most sports are about *drive phase* sprinting from 0 to 20 yards. What most athletes do incorrectly is the fast-as-possible *fly phase*, upright, sprinting technique they have been doing from the time they first learned how to run. They sprint too upright and arms pumping too tight to their bodies. The following three drills teach optimal mechanics for *drive phase* and *fly phase.*

Fly phase technique is perfect for long runs, cross-country racing, and even sprinting after 20 yards. However, using *fly phase* technique instead of *drive phase* technique means athletes will waste a lot of time taking two totally unnecessary steps during the first 10 yards.

Leg Drives Acceleration Drill

Goal: Teach optimal body positioning for drive phase acceleration

This drill is mission-critical important because it accomplishes many things needed to achieve a dramatic improvement in athletic speed performance.

The body is positioned as shown with exaggerated forward lean and called the *acceleration position*. Athletes can't accelerate fast in a upright default position discussed in Chapter 1.

The first time this drill is coached, it is important to teach several key principles of speed technique. Athletes line up leaning on the wall (or fence, or leaning on the S-Drive Treadmill) in the acceleration position. Forward lean, body straight. Both feet are back to begin the drill.

Once in the acceleration position, athletes are coached to bring right knee up toward the chest and "hold it" with ankle dorsiflexed as shown. I will generally have to go athlete to athlete and adjust the knee higher to the chest and move the foot so the ankle is the dorsiflexed position {toe up toward shin). The *athletic exercise paradox* is why I have to manually do this so athletes begin to feel the optimal speed mechanics.

Shayne Skov, NFL MLB doing leg drives Silver Creek SportsPlex San Jose CA www.gotoplex.com

Valencia Higgins demonstrates leg drives on the S-Drive self-propelled treadmill set on highest resistance level

When athletes run with *toes down and loud*, this means the brain just took the calf muscles out of the propulsion forward process because it's easier when body parts are left out of the movement so there is less muscle to oxygenate.

The *athletic exercise paradox* kicks in frequently during ankle dorsiflexion and it will have many athletes too upright. This is where the importance of the acceleration position with straight body forward is taught. Please note: Doing this drill without teaching *why this drill needs to be done* will accomplish the warm-up, but it won't teach athletes how to make self-adjustments during practice so they can accelerate faster.

Incorrect ankle dorsiflexion   *Correct ankle dorsiflexion*

Speed technique training is a speed workout, but it's not about the workout. It's about teaching athletes to become speed coaches to themselves where they can continually make adjustments to improve body mechanics during practice and training so speed technique becomes automatic during games.

When athletes run and dorsiflex their ankles with every step, this forces the recruitment of the calf muscles and the strong plantar tendons on the bottom of their feet to participate in propelling the body forward. This results in a longer stride. The *exercise paradox* is the enemy of speed training and it wants the brain to propel the movement with fewer body parts engaged to conserve energy in case it's needed later for an emergency situation.

Same applies to high knee action while in the acceleration position. Knees driving up higher toward the chest means more glute and hamstring force to propel a longer stride.

When athletes are coached to raise *right leg up and hold*, and learn ankle dorsiflexion for *drive phase* and *fly phase*, athletes will run faster that day.

When you hear an athlete run loud slapping the ground, this isn't laziness. Athletes haven't been trained in speed technique. There will be more on this when we start running in Chapter 5.

Coach Mitch Kothe adjusts the ankle during the leg drive drill so athletes feel the correct technique

31

Repeat *left leg up and hold* to make sure left ankle is now dorsiflexed and knee is going up toward the chest. Coaches will see who is very tight and actually *hamstrung*. Frequently, athletes that only do heavy squats and deadlifts without any flexibility work will have limited range of motion and their speed will be literally hamstrung. We have the fix for this condition in Chapter 10, and it only takes 10 minutes 3 days a week.

While in the acceleration position on the wall, the coaching is, *"right leg up and back, one movement, just right leg, half-speed on go."*

Three single reps each leg with a pause when feet are on the ground side-by-side. Continue the *leg drives* drill at 75% speed, right and left.

Now move to 100% speed and prepare to give the most important lecture of the day. Once you do *leg drives* at 100%, gather the group to let them know about how the *exercise paradox* impacts their speed.

Teach your athletes the brain thinks it's doing you a favor to move with slow muscle fiber leaving body parts out of the process so there is less muscle to oxygenate.

Here's what you will typically see after this speech. Athletes thought they were moving 100% speed. They weren't. Now teach athletes they have three muscle-fiber types, slow, fast and super fast. The body tries to do things with slow-muscle fiber so they can endure all day, and the brain thinks it's doing you a favor to conserve fast fiber. But athletes won't get faster unless they recruit and work all three fiber types to become stronger.

Now I explain *super-fast muscle fiber* principles (technically, type IIx or IIb) to all new athletes. The great thing about super-fast muscle is it's not meant to endure -- so you don't have to do a lot of reps -- but you do have to move as fast as you can for position-specific movements to force recruitment of this muscle fiber. When this occurs, the muscle fiber at the cellular level is traumatized, and when athletes sleep, the muscle fiber heals back bigger and stronger.

Keep doing this training three days a week and the muscle fiber propelling speed bursts will keep getting stronger and stronger. When athletes apply optimal speed technique to this process for neurological gains, athletes will keep getting faster and faster.

Explain to athletes they can become faster during the next 30 seconds if they will do this drill and make their legs move faster than they have ever moved before. With this teaching, you may see a 10 to 30% faster movement.

We aren't through with the teaching for the *leg drives* drill. After your athletes learn *muscle-fiber recruitment* how to overcome the *exercise paradox*, I bring out a one-inch band 40 inches long to explain how overspeed training works to get the neurological system firing faster and how to overcome inner-ear brakes.

We repeat the *leg drives* drill full speed except athletes place the band under their right foot (mid-point of foot is best) and place band over their right shoulder. The goal here is to *overspeed* the movement for a positive neurological adaptation by making the leg move faster than ever before with the assistance of the band.

Athletes do 3 to 5 reps per leg on "go" from a static still starting position as shown with both feet side-by-side in the forward lean acceleration position. The knee moves up and back in one movement. Every athlete should move faster.

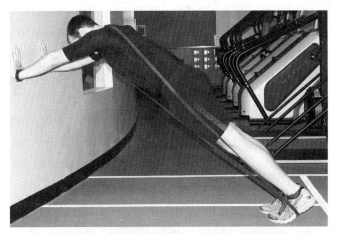

Overspeed leg drives drill demonstrated by Mitch Kothe

Every athlete should experience faster movement with the band. Frequently when the foot comes down on rep #1, the foot comes down disoriented and not where it started. This makes a great teaching point.

At the end of the drill I ask, *"Did you feel your legs move faster?"* They agree. Then I ask, *"Would you like your legs to move that fast all the time?"* Athletes smile and answer yes.

Here is the coaching point. I make this statement to athletes whether it's a pro athlete making millions or a group of 12-year old soccer athletes:

> *What I did with the band is I made your legs 5 to 8-pounds lighter. If you want to move your legs faster, you can either lose 5 to 10 pounds per leg. Not advisable. OR ... OR ... OR ... You can get your super-fast muscle fiber muscle fiber 10-pounds stronger. But you can't reach the super-fast fiber to strengthen it until you force it to be recruited by sprinting 20 yards full speed in training or practice three times a week.*

This is where the light comes on for most athletes. Even the young ones get a good understanding of the importance of practicing fast. Athletes typically become thirsty for more because they realize their work in training and practice will get them faster and faster.

 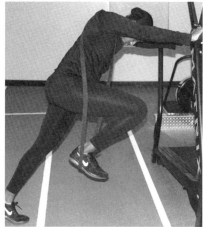

Overspeed leg drives leaning on the Matrix S-Drive with knee up high-as-possible. Up & down in one movement.
Valencia Higgins demonstrates at the
Edge Performance Center ClubSport San Jose

There is still one more mission-critical teaching point in this drill. I'll ask another question to add a new speed technique principle:

> *When you did your first rep, did you feel your leg move a little awkward and not go back to where you thought it would?*
> *The first rep was a little awkward. The second rep not as awkward, but by the third rep, you adapted and your leg was under control and it was moving much faster, wasn't it? This is what happened; your inner ear just sent messages to your brain that you are moving too fast and you could lose your balance and fall. Your brain turned on the inner-ear brakes and this made you move slower and somewhat out-of-control.*

Coaching point; It only took three reps of practice moving so fast it pushed the inner ear to a new level of balance, and it pushed the leg to move much faster. This forces the brain and nervous system to recruit maximum amounts of muscle fiber. Athletes may notice they are beginning to breathe hard. This is not because they aren't fit. It's because the heart muscle is having to work much harder to oxygenate a lot more muscle fiber.

Coach Nick Nguyen shows how Matrix S-Force places athletes in the speed-burst acceleration position for eight 15-20 seconds full-speed reps

Inner-Ear Brakes

Your inner ear does not care if you score a touchdown, beat out the throw to first, or make a game-winning tackle or catch. Your inner ear doesn't care if you get a scholarship or add millions to your contract with a low 40-yard time during the NFL Combines.

Your inner ear has one main role in life -- to keep you from falling. There are three loops in your inner ear, called semicircular canals. One canal senses up-and-down movement. Another canal senses side-to-side movement and the third canal senses tilting movements. These canals work together to sense falling and out-of-balance movements.

The inner ear is seated next to your brain and it sends powerful messages to your brain very quickly and your brain puts on speed brakes when trying to move faster. But like everything in the body that adapts to the way it's trained; the inner ear can be trained to keep the brakes off so athletes can keep getting faster and faster.

Understanding the inner-ear's role is one of the main reasons why speed technique training gets amazing and near immediate results in lower times during the first day. The concept of inner-ear brakes is taught during the Leg Drive drill and coached throughout speed technique training.

Inner-ear brakes and the *exercise paradox* should be under the constant focus of the speed coach during the first couple of speed technique training workouts until the athletes understand how to counter the enemies of speed.

How do you remove the inner-ear brakes and make every athletic movement faster? Athletes have to push their bodies out-of-balance so the inner-ear will work to provide balance when moving faster.

This needs to be an on-going coaching focus. No matter what the movement is, it can be done faster, but the inner ear has to be pushed so it adapts to new levels of speed. When using the bands as a teaching tool, we are intentionally moving faster than the inner ear is prepared so it will adapt to new levels of speed by pulling off the brakes.

Frequently, when football athletes finish the football season and play basketball, which is more of an upright jogging sport with an occasional quick 3 to 5 step sprints, athletes are shocked at how much speed they lose when they begin to sprint fast again.

Basketball does great things for vertical jump because the body adapts to the way it's trained. To run fast, you have to run fast. To jump high, you have to jump high. Basketball clearly improves vertical jump and reaching abilities, but since it resembles a cross-country sport with a lot of upright jogging (and the body adapts to the way it's trained), when a basketball player tries to sprint like he did during football season, the inner ear puts on the brakes as the athlete tries to pull forward in the acceleration position.

There is an easy fix. To keep the inner ear from putting on the brakes and maintain speed technique skills, athletes need to practice the straight body forward lean of *drive phase* for 8 reps during basketball practice three days a week or risk losing speed.

Please don't think I am against football athletes playing basketball. I am not. Basketball athletes can get faster too if they learn and apply the speed techniques in this book and sprint fast -- even if short distances -- 8 reps during basketball practice three days a week. Athletes can practice speed skill application and work their *super-fast muscle fiber* during basketball season. This will maintain fast-fiber strength and it will keep the inner ear conditioned so the speed brakes stay off.

The fastest athletes who ever lived put the most force on the ground for the least amount of time striking mid-foot

Claw Drill

Goal: Teach optimal mechanics for fly phase upright running

When we learn upright *fly phase* running, we learn to run with our feet striking the surface flat footed and loud. Coach, when you hear athletes running loud, they are either slowing down to stop, slowing down for a change-of-direction cut, or more probably; the brain is causing them to leave their strong calf muscles and the 10 muscles of the plantar structure in the bottom of the feet out of the propulsion forward process to make it easier. Your brain thinks it's doing you a favor to leave body parts out of the sprinting process so there's less to oxygenate.

The claw drill teaches the body to correctly strike the surface when in *fly phase* (upright sprinting) that occurs after the brief transition from *drive phase* to *fly phase*.

As shown below, athletes have one arm on the wall or fence for balance. Right leg is up where the thigh is parallel to the ground for the start and finish of one rep. At this point, coaches will see the *exercise paradox* kick in, as many athletes will not cock their ankles in the *leg up* position and naturally leave the toes down with ankle plantar flexed rather than dorsiflexed. Toes down plantar flexed is actually good technique for slowing down from a full-speed sprint, but it's poor technique for acceleration.

Keep the right leg up so athletes learn the feel of the correct technique as the coach adjusts the athlete's ankle if needed. Beginning at half-speed, the right leg makes a cycling movement from raised knee back up and stop with the knee raised and ankle dorsiflexed. It's not natural to dorsiflex the ankle as the knee is raised. Athletes need to learn this movement so they are using more muscle fiber to propel the movement forward. NOTE: This is not a floor stomp movement. It's a mid-foot strike leg cycle.

Correct *ankle dorsiflexion*
during claw drill on Matrix S-Drive

Correct   ***Incorrect***

While it's true the fastest athletes who ever lived put the most force on the ground, this isn't the best description of what really happens. It should be *the fastest athletes who ever lived put the most force on the ground for the least amount of time striking mid foot.* Only measuring ground force as the key marker of speed improvement may yield a false measurement of athletes improving ground force by stomping the measuring device flat footed.

You can measure more force on the ground with a flat-footed stomp, but this is contrary to optimal speed mechanics except during slow down for change-of-direction maneuvers that are frequently performed flat footed.

Most untrained athletes run with their toes pointed downward in the natural *default position*. They may appear to have fast turnover, but this is like throwing a baseball without using the wrist. There is no whip and speed is greatly reduced.

Just like the *leg drives* drill, continue the sequence of 3-5 reps per leg 50% for set one, 75% for set two, and 100% full speed on set three.

Reinforce optimal speed technique during other forms of training like Lockette Lunges (single-leg lunge jumps with a high knee) for explosive fast fiber work in the glutes, hamstrings and calves. Nationally ranked USA Masters Track & Field sprinter and jumper, Dr. Derick Phan adds ankle dorsiflexion at the top of the jump

Pocket-Chin Arms

Goal: Teach optimal arm mechanics
for drive phase and fly phase

What athletes do with their arms is perhaps the most important aspect of speed technique training. And it's the most difficult piece to master.

Pocket-chin arms drill teaches athletes the optimal arm positioning during full-speed sprinting for both *drive phase* and *fly phase.*

This drill is also called *butt bumpers* because when done correctly, athletes briefly come off the ground in a motion that resembles bumping the surface.

Arms stay *locked at 90 degrees* as shown below during the entire arm-pumping cycle. Coaches should look for no bicep-curling type movement at the top of the arm cycle. Also look for no hammering type of tricep extension during the back-arm cycle. Arms stay locked at 90 degrees for *drive phase* and *fly phase* arm pumping action.

Pocket means hands travel at least even with the back pocket on the back swing. Beyond the back pocket by several inches is desirable. Female athletes will typically find it easier to get more distance past the back pocket than males.

Chin means hands travel up to chin level on the upswing. Chin doesn't mean to touch the chin with the hand. Arms stay locked at 90 degrees with hands traveling high to *chin level* 8-12 inches away from the chin as shown.

Pocket-chin arms drill demonstrated by coach Valencia Higgins

Athletes sit with feet in front, straight and locked. After the coach checks for the correct arm positioning, the first command for this drill is *pocket-chin arms, half-speed, go*. Make sure technique is correct at 50% speed before going to 75% speed for 5 seconds, and then full speed for 5 seconds.

The default position for the *exercise paradox* (to make the arm-pumping movement easier) is *pocket-chest arms* with arms too tight to the chest rather than *pocket-chin arms* (shown below by coach Valencia Higgins). We learn how to run with *pocket-chest* mechanics to stay too upright in slow-fiber recruitment mode as this keeps our inner-ear's need for balance happy, and it makes it easier.

Some athletes get part of the movement correct, but then add a little bicep curl at the end of the arm upswing to stay in the *pocket-chest* pattern. Arms too close to the chest makes athletes take too many unnecessary TIME-CONSUMING steps. In over 30 years, I can't remember one athlete I've worked with that didn't take two unnecessary steps the first 10 yards. This includes several athletes with Super Bowl rings.

Pocket-chin arms starts the process to teach this mission critical speed technique. Whether an athlete is on the third step or the thirtieth step of a linear sprint, the arms always stay locked 90 degrees and pumping back pocket to chin level. *Pocket-chest arms* is the natural movement pattern, but it is the enemy of speed.

Pocket-chin arms drill - standing

*Pocket-chin arms drill on the Matrix S-Drive
demonstrated by Zac Elliott*

Optimal Arm Swing Mechanics

In addition to the arms traveling from back pocket to chin level, the arms also travel slightly toward the center line of the body on the upswing while keeping *elbows locked at 90 degrees*. The center of the body line is also called the median line or the midsagittal plane to represent the midline running down the center of the body from front to back.

When arms travel toward the center line, this movement maximizes stride length by allowing the hips to slightly rotate. Arm pumping action during full-speed sprinting movements controls the hips. Correct technique during *pocket-chin arms* is demonstrated below by coach Chris Wulff, ClubSport San Jose and former university strength & conditioning coach.

Correct pocket-chin arms
*Hands travel toward the center line of the body to chin level
with hands 8-12 inches away from the chin*

Under Rotating the Hips Error

Under rotating the hips is more frequently seen in male athletes, especially those with tight hips. While Carl Lewis popularized the knife hand as it was shown on national television with millions watching, his arms still came toward the center and above his jaw line to get optimal hip rotation. When demonstrating running form on You Tube, his arms would stay wider than when he actually ran races. If you watch film of one of the greatest male track athletes of all time, during Olympic races from the front view, you will see his upswing arm moving toward the center line of the body, and his hands would pass chin level on the upswing as shown in the optimal technique arm-pumping position on page 45.

A straight knife hand is fine during a sprint, although I recommend to football receivers to separate fingers slightly to better prepare hands for catching. Many people think the technique shown below is correct. It is not. Not having the arms move toward the center line of the body under rotates the hips and shortens stride length.

__Incorrect__ pocket-chin arms
This arm action under rotates the hips

Over Rotating the Hips Error

Over rotating the hips during arm pumping action is a serious error. Over rotation can be actually dangerous to ACL knee ligaments.

Crossing over the center line during the arm upswing as shown below makes the hips over rotate and this shortens stride length for a slower sprint, and it can place the ACLs in a vulnerable valgus position.

The arm pumping movement pattern controls the hips. This incorrect arm movement pattern can become a major issue for coaches with female athletes.

***Incorrect** pocket-chin arms*
This arm action over rotates the hips

The same reason many female athletes naturally do valgus squats (with knees in) is due to the brain trying to use leverage from the skeleton to accomplish the squat and make it easier on muscles (*exercise paradox*).

Female athletes will frequently land after a jump in a valgus position, which is dangerous to the knee ligaments. In fact, the ACL test for female athletes is to have them step off a bench in front of a mirror and observe what their knees do naturally when they land.

Female athletes landing *valgus* will be looking at a potential ACL replacement after age 40 when female ACLs begin to get smaller and weaker UNLESS they learn how to jump and land without their knees going inward to the *valgus position*.

Correct squatting form can help teach female athletes to avoid a valgus knee position. Whether it's a front squat or back squat with barbell, dumbbells or kettlebells, the knees should not move into a valgus position as shown below. Whether it's an ass-to-grass squat or parallel squat, the knees should not be moving inward, but staying out and traveling in the same plane over the toes.

Incorrect - *Knees moving inward in valgus position*

I can't emphasize enough the importance of the three speed technique drills in Chapter 3. Everything done in speed training reflects what is taught to athletes during the initial Speed Technique 101 session that focuses on these three drills.

I suggest multitasking and making these three drills, *leg drives*, *claw drill* and *pocket-chin arms* part of the *specific warm-up* before every practice. If you do, your athletes will play the video game of perfect speed technique in the brain before practice. If they practice faster than normal, they recruit more fast twitch IIa and IIx muscle fiber to keep getting stronger and stronger and faster and faster all season long.

Speed training is like driving on the freeway going 90 MPH, and game speed, 70 MPH seems slow. Do speed technique training early in the practice and I can just about guarantee you'll see your team practice faster.

Correct - *knees over toes and knees moving in direction of the toes*

*Middle Linebacker Shayne Skov
preparing for the coming NFL season.*

*Nine-year NFL starting safety Marlon McCree
multitasking pocket-chin arms technique practice
during drive phase bleacher lunges*

4

The Acceleration Ladder

Once the speed technique skills have been mastered in pieces, the acceleration ladder is used to begin putting the pieces together as athletes begin to run. I walk athletes to the 3/4 point of the ladder where they will be soon running to check their body mechanics. The 3/4 point in the ladder is approximately 8 yards from the start line.

Once athletes have mastered *pocket-chin arms* on the floor, they will do the same drill standing up in the ladder. If in a team setting or small group, athletes line up in a straight line 8 yards from the start line.

They are instructed to place their bodies in optimal speed position to propel the body with the fastest muscle fiber in the body. Coaches are looking for a straight body, chin down, forward lean.

I will question; *Am I straight up with my arms pocket chest, or am I leaning forward with a straight body from head to toe with elbows locked at 90 degrees and arms moving pocket to chin level?*

Athletes repeat the *standing pocket-chin arms* drill beginning at 50% speed for a few seconds (as coaches check their technique), then 75% speed for a few seconds, and full speed to finish with a countdown *5, 4, 3, 2, 1.*

Did you feel your body try to move forward, and almost have to fight to keep from falling forward? I'll ask this question to make a point; the arms alone will pull the body forward even without moving the legs.

Pocket-chin arms standing at 3/4 point of the acceleration ladder

I will ask a follow-up question; *Did that rep get you more winded than you thought?* It always does, and here's the point. Athletes just did an upper-body sprint. It's a hard rep because there's a lot of muscle to oxygenate in the upper body when forcing the recruitment of all three muscle-fiber types to propel the upper-body component of sprinting.

I will explain when the legs are added, true full-speed sprinting is extremely demanding on the body and this is why most athletes don't practice full speed. They may think they are full speed, but it's generally 80 to 90 percent speed.

If athletes will sprint hard and fast as possible for 20 yards during practice, this will recruit all three fiber types and create micro-trauma in their muscles so when they sleep, all three fiber types grow bigger and stronger. Their fast-muscle fiber will get stronger, but this also means coaches are accomplishing both kinds of conditioning for sports -- aerobic conditioning and anaerobic conditioning.

Until the heart muscle is having to work hard attempting to oxygenate quite literally twice the muscle fiber, it may be hard, but it's slow-twitch hard. Running cross country is hard, but it won't make athletes faster for sprinting sports.

Pocket-chin arms standing at midpoint of the acceleration ladder

Athletes move to midpoint in the ladder (5 yards from start line) for the next rep. I will ask a similar question. *How are you going to position your body at this point in the ladder to propel the movement with the fastest, strongest muscle in the body as your body starts low and slowly begins coming up like an airplane taking off?* Athletes are almost always on board at this point and move right into the correct positioning for the next section of the drill.

Athletes now come to the hardest part of the final drill before they actually begin sprinting through the ladder -- the second to third step after the start.

The body is very low and straight, chin down and arms are in exaggerated *pocket-chin arms* (shown below) for a 50%, 75% and full-speed rep with a *5, 4, 3, 2, 1* count from the coach.

It is very difficult for athletes to maintain their balance moving full speed in this awkward position, which means they are pushing the inner ear to a new level it's not accustomed to -- intentionally.

Just like everything in the body, the inner ear adapts to the way it's trained. The way to improve balance for a position-specific movement is to push the inner ear out-of-balance via moving faster than ever before with optimal technique and fight to regain balance. After just a couple of reps, the inner ear begins to adapt and athletes will move faster because the brain removes the inner-ear brakes.

Pocket-chin arms at the second step in the acceleration ladder

Now athletes are ready to sprint in the ladder. I don't sell acceleration ladders, nor do I get commission for recommending them, but it is perhaps the most valuable tool in the speed technique arsenal because it teaches athletes how to eliminate two unnecessary steps during the first 10 yards.

This ladder is extremely useful for the fastest athletes on the team, as naturally fast athletes typically lose time popping up into *fly phase* too soon.

The more anxious an athlete is the more likely he/she is to pop up into *fly phase* and take two or more unnecessary steps

The first rung is set 6 to 8 inches past the start line and gradually moved out so the first step is longer. The following rung measurements serve as a guide for adult athletes to teach how quickly they must lengthen their strides. Naturally fast athletes want to feel the *tap tap tap* of feet moving fast, which means they are quite literally spinning their wheels and taking too many steps to cover distance.

Rung

1	0″
2	28″
3	38″
4	46″
6	60″
7	60″
8	70″

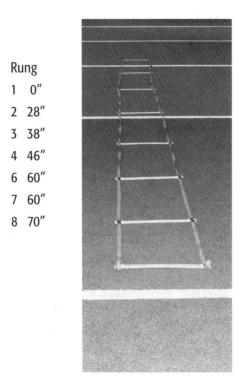

Note: the first rung of the ladder shown is 6-8 inches past the starting line. Depending on age and speed of athletes, length to the first rung will be gradually adjusted for a desirable longer first step

Fast football athletes will cover 100 meters in 46 to 50 steps. Experienced Olympic 100-meter sprinters will cover the distance in around 44 steps. Usain Bolt takes 41 steps to cover 100 meters. He achieves this NOT by coming up too fast into *fly phase* technique and reaching and pulling for stride length. He focuses on optimal speed technique and the by-product of the technique eliminates unnecessary steps.

Athletes who perform timed drills in the least number of steps with good technique will typically score the fastest times.

Jackson Christian School soccer team working on speed technique during the season. The Speed Technique Start is used to teach soccer athletes correct acceleration form for short quick-burst sprints

5

The Start

Athletes are close to being ready to sprint full speed once the starting technique is covered. The start is added after the *General Warm-up* and *Specific Warm-up*, which includes the three main speed technique drills.

The *Speed Technique Start* (or *Combine Start*) is a three-point down stance and it is used for every athlete during speed technique training. This also applies to athletes in sports that don't start in a down start like soccer, softball, baseball, lacrosse and basketball because it forces athletes to learn how to position their body in acceleration position by pushing the inner ear out of its comfort zone.

The first goal of the start is to reprogram the brain and inner ear so athletes learn they won't fall when they hit the straight body, chin down, forward-lean acceleration position while moving full speed.

The combine start is also taught with the purpose of training athletes how to position the body to propel the sprinting movement forward that resembles an airplane taking off -- straight body, chin down, slowly coming up as athletes sprint through *drive phase* rather than the natural tendency (caused by the *exercise paradox*) of popping up too upright and into *fly phase* too soon.

This start is very close to a falling start when used for training purposes. When used for formal time testing, athletes should be required to freeze two seconds before starting.

The athlete is close to the starting line as possible. The hips are higher than the shoulders. Head is down. The athlete's up hand is NOT up past the body to improve hand-timing accuracy. If the hand is up higher than the body, the timer sees the hand movement first, and the clock starts before the athlete is actually sprinting. If electronic timing is used, the hand-to-the-side method isn't as important

NOTE: This isn't a comfortable starting position. It is somewhat uncomfortable to help athletes make an explosive, violent start using every muscle fiber in the body to propel the body forward, not upward but forward. This starting position is to force athletes to spring out of the starting position similar to diving into a swimming pool pushing off with both feet. The goal is to NOT jump upward off of one foot. Rather, it is to dive forward using both feet.

When athletes start with a one-foot push, this is called a *walking start*, and it is very slow compared to a speed start, which uses both feet diving forward.

There is a system to position athletes in the combine starting position. First, have athletes stand with feet under their shoulders and just behind the line.

Begin with both feet behind the line

Pull one foot back 12 inches or less and drop the hand to the ground to create a triangle as shown below.

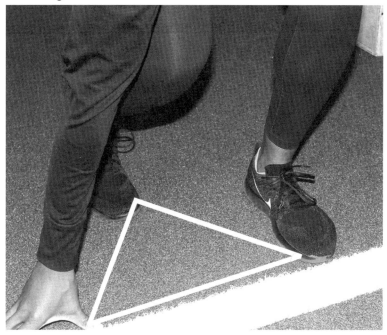

Create the starting triangle

The above is a classical combine starting position; however, the goal of speed technique training is not to perform a classical start. The purpose is to create a speed improving start by pushing the inner ear to a new level of balance and force the brain to release the inner-ear brakes. This is accomplished by getting lots of body weight forward to create a near-falling start. Athletes are instructed to place the up hand (left) out in front as shown below and put weight on that hand.

Athletes are now instructed to slowly bring the hand that is out (left hand) slowly to the athlete's hip.

Once the hand reaches the hip as shown below and without pausing, the same (left) arm that is moving is thrown forward for a near-falling momentum start -- diving forward, head down, pushing off with both feet as if diving into a swimming pool. Athletes typically do not fall at the start because the back leg comes up very fast (probably faster than it has moved in a start before).

Athletes are instructed to use the combine start and sprint through the ladder before slowing down. Not the whole 20 yards. Rep #1 is 50% speed.

Here I will explain to athletes 50% is 100% minus some. 50% is faster than many athletes think, otherwise the first rep becomes a 30% intensity rep. The *exercise paradox* seems to appear on every new movement to make it easier.

The goal is to hug the line as close as possible. Large athletes may need to move feet back by one step as shown by Shayne Skov at Silver Creek SportsPlex San Jose

The next rep is 75% to 90% speed depending on ambient conditions and the constant assessment of hamstrings. I am constantly asking; *how do your hamstrings feel?* If hamstrings are sore to touch at this point, athletes should not sprint full speed.

The last skill-applying ramp-up rep is 100% full speed to the end of the ladder because we are still conserving energy for several full-speed timed 20-yard reps.

If an athlete starts out-of-balance and sprints through the ladder and the first 2 or 3 steps become a slight stumble or out-of-balance, *celebrate the athlete's willingness to push the body and the inner ear to a new level of speed the body isn't accustomed to -- yet.*

Before an athlete can speed up a movement, typically the athlete has to be willing to push the body so fast the first 2 or 3 reps are out-of-balance. This concept was discussed in detail with the leg drive dill in Chapter 3.

During functional, position-specific speed training where the down start isn't used, coaches will clearly see athletes using significantly improved acceleration body mechanics and better forward lean. The stimulus for the improvement happens during the speed technique drills and the acceleration ladder sprints.

Note: If I have new athletes flying in for Speed Technique 101 and 102, I'll time a baseline 20 at this point -- from the athletes' first movement to the 20-yard finish line. This performance is charted on one page so other athletes do not see other's times. Speed technique isn't about comparing times with other athletes. Speed technique training is about creating a *you vs. you learning environment* so every athlete lives up to his or her speed potential.

Before the timing begins, I'll explain that sharing times is counterproductive. By now, athletes are serious and focused. They typically do not share times with this instruction.

After an athlete sprints the baseline 20, I'll show each athlete his or her time. After every timed rep, the athlete walks back to me, sees the new time vs. the baseline 20, and hears a coaching tip based on that one rep.

Athletes will typically see numbers on a clip board with their one-page documenting improvement over several timed reps. This also reinforces the fact that working hard to learn new technique and applying new speed knowledge will yield performance improvement on almost every rep.

Advanced ladder start with an extended long first step demonstrated by former college track sprinter and high school track coach Christine Campbell

6

Strategic Acceleration Bursts

There are two opportunities to accelerate in a 20-yard sprint. The first one is at the start and the second is at the 12 to 15-yard mark when coming out of the acceleration ladder. Most athletes know about the start, but over the years, I have only seen one athlete who knew about the second acceleration point. He was a pro athlete trained by Remi Korchemi, a well-known speed technique coach who defected from communist Russia to come to the U.S. after the 1972 Olympics.

Unless athletes have been through an elite speed technique training program with a coach who knows speed technique, they probably do not know they are leaving a huge acceleration opportunity out of the process at the 12-yard point when running a 20 or 40-yard sprint, or a baseball showcase 60.

The ladder teaches athletes how to eliminate two unnecessary steps during the first 10 yards, and it also teaches athletes where the second acceleration point is and how quickly it arrives.

Once athletes have timed a baseline 20-yard sprint, I'll kid them, *the next technique is so powerful it can kill you.* This always gets their attention.

Valsalva Turbo-Burst Acceleration

This technique is one of the most powerful techniques in all of sports because it increases your blood pressure significantly and takes your body to peak maximal effort that only last a few brief seconds.

This technique is performed by most athletes naturally. When a soccer athlete kicks a hard corner kick, it is frequently used. When a linebacker makes a tackle, this technique is used. When a center fielder catches a hopper near the fence and sees the runner rounding second headed for third and the center fielder unleashes everything possible to make the throw, it is used. A boxer throwing a hard-left hook going for the knockout, this technique is used. It is used because it works.

Recently, it has become fashionable for tennis athletes to yell (or kiai) on every shot. Why? Because when they do, they hit much harder by tapping into a natural physiological process of the body that takes the body to peak maximal effort that only lasts approximately two seconds.

This technique is called the *Valsalva Maneuver*. You may have heard you should never do the Valsalva when exercising. You have heard it before, *breathe when you exercise*. I have heard this hundreds of times over the years. Why are people taught to *breathe when you exercise* in the first place? Here's why. When you *don't*, this causes a momentary increase in blood pressure, which can be potentially dangerous especially for nursing home residents and those who are at high-risk for stroke. But this is exactly what young healthy athletes do all the time to take their body to peak maximal effort. Researchers report:

> *During resistance exercise, a brief Valsalva Maneuver (VM) is unavoidable when lifting heavy loads . . . The VM was associated with an increase in blood pressure during resistance exercise, but the VM alone was associated with greater hemodynamic changes. In conclusion, the VM effectively increases IAP* (intra-abdominal pressure), *which may assist with spine stability and trunk rigidity during resistance exercise,*
> (Hackett, D., 2013. *The Valsalva Maneuver: Its Effect on Intra-abdominal Pressure and Safety Issues During Resistance Exercise*. J Strength & Conditioning Research: August 2013. Volume 27. #8. pp 2338–2345 doi: 10.1519/JSC.0b013e31827de07d).

Athletes do a personal test at this point. I ask them to simulate doing a squat and bench max, except inhale on the way up. They quickly see they can't take the body to peak maximal effort when inhaling.

Try this personal test, simulate you are kicking a 50-yard field goal, except inhale as you make the kicking movement. Simulate throwing a baseball, center field to home, except inhale as you make the throwing motion. Or bend forward to make a tackle, except inhale at the moment of impact. You should realize you have been using this technique all your life.

Women giving birth do the Valsalva. Every time you have a bowel movement, the Valsalva was probably used. But we are taught *breathe when you exercise*. And you should breathe when you exercise. But know the human body has a method to go to peak maximal effort that last a few short seconds and athletes need to know where, when and how to apply this very powerful technique.

The formal definition of Valsalva Maneuver is *a forceful attempt at expiration when the airway is closed at some point.* This happens for a brief moment to start the process before a grunt or a full- fledged kiai yell. The Valsalva begins with violently tightening the ab muscles.

In a major study, researchers conclude: *The velocity, force, and peak muscle activity during tennis serves and forehand strokes are significantly enhanced when athletes are allowed to grunt,* (O'Connell, D. 2014 *The Effects of "Grunting" on Serve and Forehand Velocity in Collegiate Tennis Players* June 2014 . J Strength & Conditioning Research 28 (12).

Using this powerful 1 to 2-second technique produced measurable velocity improvements of 4.9% in the tennis serve and 5.31% in the forehand.

Hand grip was studied in *Something to Shout About: A Simple, Quick Performance Enhancement Technique Improved Strength in Both Experts and Novices.* This study demonstrated that hand grip increased by 7%, (Amy S. Welch & Mark Tschampl (2012) *Something to Shout About: A Simple, Quick Performance Enhancement Technique Improved Strength in Both Experts and Novices, Journal of Applied Sport Psychology,* 24:4, 418-428, DOI: 10.1080/10413200.2012.688787).

Researchers Ikai and Steinhaus investigated years ago if shouting could increase the force applied to a cable tensiometer. They showed force increased by 12% during an isometric forearm flexor task when shouting, (Ikai, M. 1961 *Some factors modifying the expression of human strength.* J Applied Physiology. 1961 Jan 1;16(1):157–63).

What does this technique do for kicking sports like martial arts, soccer and field goal kicking? A 2018 study shows a measurable 9% increase in force, (Sinnett, S. 2018.. *Grunting's competitive advantage: Considerations of force and distraction* February 22, 2018. https://doi.org/10.1371/journal.pone.0192939).

Where does this extra force come from that can increase velocity in hard athletic movements by 4 to 12%?

During a brief Valsalva Phase I, the heart rate decreases, but *blood pressure rises* substantially as shown below. The combination of 1 to 2 seconds of violent abs and briefly holding your breath is how the human body goes to peak max effort. If you hold your breath for much longer (phase II Valsalva), blood pressure begins to drop as shown. If you keep straining and holding your breath while in Valsalva Phase II for longer than a few seconds, blood pressure continues to drop and you can pass out.

Valsalva impact on blood pressure & heart rate

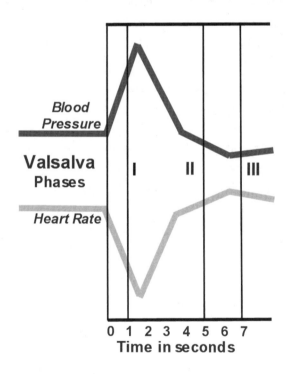

Klabunde, Richard. *Hemodynamics of a Valsalva Maneuver,* Cardiovascular Physiology Concepts. *https://www.cvphysiology.com/ Hemodynamics/H014. htm*

Fighter pilots also use this technique. It's called the Anti-G Straining Maneuver (AGSM) and commonly called the *Hook Maneuver*. When pilots are flying fast with so much G-Force they can pass out, this unclassified technique is used. Fighter pilots breathe in and violently tighten their abs and strain. Then they say the word *Hook* drawing out the *K* sound for 3 seconds. Inhale and repeat several times until the blood pressure normalizes to the G-Force, (*https://gearpatrol.com/2017/10/04/hook-maneuver-agsm-tutorial/*).

This is a powerful technique and a great tool for athletes to use to help propel acceleration bursts.

The key to this powerful technique in sports is the strategic timing of when and how long to use it. The best description I have found to communicate this technique to athletes to use during a short quick burst of speed is to breathe like a swim sprinter -- *stroke, stroke, quick slip of air, stroke, stroke.*

Briefly holding the breath is only part of an athletic Valsalva. Athletes *don't have to yell* or grunt, but they do have to violently tighten their abs muscles. When this happens together, it propels the body with maximal force applied for any quick, brief athletic movement like kicking, pitching, starting from the combine start, or a fast change-of-direction cutting movement.

To teach the *Valsalva Turbo Gear,* athletes put their right hand on their ab muscles and push; followed by, *When I say go, you yell GO with me as loud as you can and notice what your ab muscles do. Ready. Set. GO!*

Athletes are asked, *What did your abs do?*

They will generally say, *They tighten up* or *flexed.*

I realize this will be controversial for some coaches and parents. It shouldn't be because this is what the body does naturally to go to peak max effort so the human body can move faster with more force.

The Valsalva technique is added to the first acceleration point during the start and practiced for a few full-speed sprint reps through the ladder.

Note: While we just timed a baseline 20, athletes aren't sprinting the whole 20 yards as this technique is being added to the speed arsenal. Athletes are learning a new technique and conserving energy for several timed 20-yard reps once the two acceleration points in the 20 are mastered. They are using this technique for the hard all-out start for the first three to five steps, then coasting through the ladder.

The athlete gets into the combine starting position breathing normally with hand up as demonstrated by NFL linebacker Shayne Skov at the Silver Creek SportsPlex, San Jose California (*https://gotoplex.com*).

Next, the athlete exhales slowly as he/she lowers the hand to the ground to put weight on it for a brief moment. The athlete SLOWLY raises the same (left) hand up to the hip without pausing while inhaling to fill the lungs. When the (left) hand reaches the hip, the athlete violently tightens the abs and throws the arm forward (aiming knee level one body length away) as if diving into a swimming pool using the Valsalva acceleration technique to take the body to peak max effort during the start.

Because there is approximately 10% more force in this starting technique, athletes will typically lose their balance the first rep or two. This out-of-balance start is to be celebrated as they are willing to push their bodies to a new level of speed that their inner ear isn't accustomed to yet.

Athletes will feel the power of this technique. Some will clearly be out-of-balance and can't run in a straight line. Some athletes may run one or two steps outside the ladder. But just like the assisted leg drive drill with bands, it only takes a few reps to train the inner ear this start can be performed much faster without falling.

After 2 to 4 reps, the combine start is somewhat mastered (move on after 4 reps are performed). Athletes now move to the second acceleration point coming out of the ladder. This acceleration point has huge value once athletes learn the technique because it teaches them how to accelerate during many different athletic movements. Once this technique is mastered, it will give athletes a tool for pull-away speed.

I walk athletes to the end of the ladder to explain the opportunity they have to apply their new speed skill at this strategic acceleration point that most people don't know exists.

Speed skill is applied knowledge that athletes are obtaining with every rep, but they have to be running full speed to learn the correct technique video game in the brain. Athletes can't learn this technique running slow.

Every rep in speed technique training should be more than anaerobic conditioning. It should be technique execution and reinforcement of optimal speed technique as well as conditioning.

The goal of this acceleration point is to keep athletes in *drive phase* acceleration longer and keep them from getting upright in *fly phase* with arms pumping *pocket chest* rather than *pocket chin* so stride length is maximized.

This acceleration point is the most important one to get right because most athletic movements aren't done from a static-still starting position.

Once this acceleration technique is performed correctly full speed, the goal then becomes to practice the optimal technique video game in the brain and begin rewriting default (of the *exercise paradox* method of popping up too quickly).

With the athletes at the end of the ladder, I'll explain that sports commentators are always talking about fast athletes with *another gear* or *another level of speed*, which is simply using the technique of tapping into the same physiological process they just learned in the start to take the body to peak maximal effort. Now they are applying the same technique coming out of the ladder that they learned during the explosive start.

In essence, athletes are trying to do two max reps of effort back-to-back and driving the blood pressure up twice for two accelerations bursts during a 20-yard sprint.

At this point, athletes practice a couple of reps with two acceleration bursts and sprint the full 20 yards. Once they work through some inner-ear issues applying the second acceleration point, we will time the 20 with new technique.

What coaches will see the first rep or two, the inner ear will send the arms back to default *pocket-chest* rather than *pocket-chin arms* as they hit the hard violent abs acceleration burst coming out of the ladder.

Some athletes have never had their head pop up with chin up toward the sky. But the inner ear is powerful, and even though they have never done this before, the inner ear will throw the chin-up, head-back brakes to slow down the acceleration burst. Coaches will see different ways the brain puts on speed brakes.

We move next to timing reps that focus on one technique aspect per rep. The first couple of timed reps, *pocket-chin arms* will be the focus. Once progress is made and the arms aren't *pocket chest*, the focus then becomes adding the *violent abs acceleration technique*. Coaches will see, and athletes will feel, new levels of speed as they begin to put the technique pieces together.

I'll add a few tips along the way to improve the test-taking aspect of timing. I explain the *baseball curse* during the timed 20s. *Baseball curse* impacts every baseball and softball athlete significantly, and most other sports as well.

Baseball and softball athletes have spent years training the body to slow down before reaching the base to make the turn toward second. In many respects, these athletes have been playing a video game in the brain to slow down before the finish line.

Every, and I mean every, baseball athlete I've worked with stops two to three steps before the finish line in a showcase 60. Have you ever seen football athletes throw the ball down just before getting into the end zone? I promise you, they think they are in the end zone. They are shocked when they see the replay. What happened is the *exercise paradox* kicked in and they stopped too soon.

The *exercise paradox* is very powerful and just telling yourself to *run through* the finish line doesn't work. Athletes have to quite literally fake their brain off and visualize the timer is three steps beyond the finish line. Otherwise, most athletes will stop one or more steps before the finish line, and baseball athletes will stop two or three steps short.

Coach, you can hear this happening. You'll hear quick, somewhat quiet tap tap tap during sprinting, but when you hear a loud, flat-footed step one or two steps before the finish line, this means the runner's brain said, *stop, I'm finished. Exercise paradox* strikes again.

Adam November working on drive phase

During the two timed reps focusing on *pocket-chins arms*, athletes will typically see their 20 times improve with every rep. The goal of the timing reps isn't just to improve 20 times. The goal is master new speed technique while sprinting full speed where it counts.

Every timed rep helps to reprogram the brain to play the correct technique video game faster and faster. Once speed technique becomes consistent at full speed, it will become speed skill when athletes perform optimal speed mechanics without thinking about it.

This doesn't happen during Speed 101 and 102. It happens once athletes know speed technique and go home to practice speed technique three times a week. Speed technique training, as I wrote at the beginning of the book, isn't about the workout. It is a workout, but it's about teaching athletes to become a speed coach to themselves so they can continue making slight adjustments as they continue to get faster and faster.

If an athlete doesn't push himself or herself out-of-balance performing a position-specific movement and so fast the inner ear can't handle the balance, this is a sign the athlete isn't getting faster. Every athletic movement can become faster but athletes have to be willing to push the body out-of-balance moving at a new level of speed.

The next focus area for a timed 20 is the *violent abs* rep. I'll explain this rep; *even if it's a slower time, that's okay, but make your abs violent as possible at the start and again coming out of the ladder. I mean violent. Violent like you have to get there to save your mom's life.*

I'll also show them a photo of Maurice Green, one of the fastest 60m sprinters of all times. And I'll ask if they see him relaxed. His face isn't relaxed. It's intense as intense can be. While we don't want the shoulders up and tense, sprinting is violent. The term *relaxation* is a great term for endurance athletes who need to relax and NOT recruit fast fiber so there is less muscle to oxygenate. Sprinting short distances is about violence and forcing fast-fiber recruitment.

I then pull out some photos of LoLo Jones, the famous US hurdler. I show athletes she has a beautiful smile when she was on the Tonight Show. I'll then flip to the page with photos of her competing. There is no relaxation in her face. There is violence.

I'll add, *you can be the nicest person with your friends and smile, but sprinting short distances is violent. We are trying to force the brain to recruit every muscle fiber in your body to propel the sprint faster than ever before.*

Personally, I prefer the coaching description of *relying on technique* rather than the word *relaxation*. Relying on technique is important in *fly phase* upright running. Sprinting is violent. Sprinting requires *violent abs* to pull the body forward in acceleration position and stay in *drive phase* longer.

The second acceleration burst opportunity is coming out of the ladder, where it's very easy to allow the arms to go back to *pocket chest* rather than keeping *pocket-chin arms* technique when hitting this acceleration point. It takes practice to get these two techniques working together in harmony. But when they do, oh my, it's so much faster.

After the *violent abs* acceleration burst teaching, the next rep is timed. Not always, but frequently, this will be the fastest rep thus far. Even if they don't hit the optimal *pocket-chin arms* technique perfectly, the *violent abs* rep can still be faster. We may do two reps to keep refining the *violent abs* focused rep.

The last timed 20 rep is the *rely on technique rep*. Before this rep, I'll explain; *focus on optimal technique even if it seems slower. Do an optimal speed technique rep. Think about being a speed coach to yourself. Body straight like an airplane taking off -- head down, chin down, pocket-chin arms. You have two opportunities to accelerate with violent abs propelling two speed bursts, and remember the baseball curse at the end.*

It's all beginning to come together at this point. The coaching here is to set up the last 20-yard sprint as a recap of all the speed techniques they have learned thus far during the linear speed component of Speed 101. The great majority of the time, this will be the fastest rep.

When athletes learn how to focus on correct technique, not relax, but *rely on technique*, most athletes will run their fastest 20 ever. Most athletes are now covering 20 yards in the same amount of time they were covering 15 to 16 yards before they completed Speed Technique 101 linear training.

Fly Phase Flying 20s

The most important part for sports, the 20-yard sprint has been covered in drive phase. Flying 20s are next. The flying 20 represents the second part of the 40, and it also represents the second and third part of the baseball showcase 60. We only do two reps during 101 because the athlete's fast fiber is just about gone.

Two reps do not master this part of the 40-yard sprint, but it applies the speed technique learned during the *drive phase* 20 to the *fly phase* 20. This will need to be practiced at home.

A flying 20 begins with a 10-yard ramp up from a 50% speed standing start and hits full speed before the flying 20 starting point. The timer starts the clock when the athlete is full speed at the mark and stops 20-yards later. This aspect of hand timing is never perfectly accurate for flying 20s, but it's generally close, and it provides a baseline for improvement benchmarking.

Athletes are coached to be at full speed at the cone a few yards before the actual flying 20-yard start line and they hit a second acceleration burst at the next cone, which is 10 to 12 yards from the finish line.

There are three potential acceleration points in the 40-yard sprint. First is the start. The second is at the 10 to 12-yard mark (coming out of the acceleration ladder), and the last one is 10 to 12 yards away from the 40-finish line.

Invariably, when athletes run their first flying 20, I know what the reaction will be before they run. They are almost shocked, but this rep will feel like a foreign event where they are out-of-balance and control. Their brains have been playing the optimal technique 20-yard sprint video game for 1.5 hours, and now the video game has totally changed. Here is where I explain the video game concept and the need to practice full speed three days a week when they get back home.

The second rep is more comfortable and faster. By this point, they generally know where their mistakes are. I'll ask, *what did your arms do? What happened when you hit the acceleration burst? Did the baseball curse kick in that time?* The goal is to get athletes to begin accepting responsibility for their speed work when they get home.

I don't typically time 40s because athletes are so prejudice that if they can't run a 4.3, they are slow. The goal of speed technique is to help every athlete live up to his or her speed potential. In Ricardo Lockette's case, it was a 4.28.

If you visit my website *www.40speed.com* and look for *Scenes from Speed Camp*, you will see hundreds of athletes I have worked with over the years.

You'll see Julian Edelman and Ricardo Lockette, two receivers with perfect speed technique who played against each other in Super Bowl 2015. Both have several Super Bowl rings. Julian was named Super Bowl MVP in the 2019 Super Bowl, and the second in MVP voting during the 2017 Super Bowl. You may remember he made an unbelievable catch that has been called *the greatest catch in Super Bowl history.*

With 22 seconds left in the 2015 Super Bowl, Ricardo Lockette playing against Julian had a shot at the catch to win the game. Jermaine Kearse set the pick. Ricardo ran a quick slant to win the game, but the Patriots were prepared for the play and Malcolm Butler made what has been called *the greatest defensive play in Super Bowl history* by intercepting the pass to win the game.

Ricardo has run the fastest 40 I've ever seen, 4.28. He ran three reps at this extremely fast time with two coaches timing before I would believe it. I have had several athletes over the years tell me they have run under 4.3. I have seen less than a hand full of these blazing fast times.

Julian Edelman was the fastest young athlete I've ever seen. I remember talking to his dad Frank and saying if they don't give Julian a shot in high school football because of his size, he is fast enough to run track in college.

That changed when Nick Nicolopulos became the head football coach at Woodside High School, Woodside California. He gave this small but extremely fast, smart, and focused QB a shot. I had the privilege of coaching a two-day speed technique camp for this team before the season.

Julian led his team to a 13 and 0 perfect season and during the championship game, this team with a record of 2 and 8 the prior year, made big plays when they were needed, and they won. Coach Nick said about Julian, *He always came up big when we needed it.* And he is still doing this today. If you observe film of Julian during a sprint on a straight stretch, you should see him demonstrate optimal speed technique with *pocket-chin arms* and straight-body forward lean.

Julian was drafted in the 7th round because of his size at a draft number that's considered almost guaranteed not to make it. Ricardo Lockette was passed over in the draft.

Another undrafted, small, but blazing fast speed-technique athlete, Jabari Greer, retired with the New Orleans Saints after a 10-year NFL career.

Jabari Greer established a non-profit foundation, the Greer Campaign, that is focused on programs to assist single and married fathers in developing their parenting skills. Jabari, Julian and Ricardo all have Super Bowl rings.

In the *Scenes from Speed Camp* section at *www.40speed.com*, you'll see numerous high school athletes needing two tenths to have the speed necessary to play at the next level. A great many of these athletes do pick up two tenths from speed technique training. And when they go back home and practice optimal technique, they keep getting faster and faster. Many have received scholarships and played the game they love in college.

Here are just a few stories of how learning speed technique can change a young person's life.

Ben Beckwith, high school freshman (Benton MS) with dad, Wayne Keith McBride (Collierville, TN) with dad Keith

Ben Beckwith high school Soph, and dad returning for refresher speed technique with football athletes Jordan Davis, and Jacob Davis

Ben Beckwith high school junior year used his speed skills to steal bases in baseball. In football, at 300 pounds, 6'5" Big Ben has been breaking records. Photo with Dad, Wayne, who traveled a long way every summer for two days of speed technique training during Ben's high school years

Ben Beckwith worked on speed technique consistently for years and walked on at Mississippi State. He earned a starting position. I was told the head coach would run Ben with the Linebackers to show them how fast a lineman can run if they work hard. Along with QB Dak Prescott, they took their SEC team to #1 in the nation for several weeks. After graduating, Ben played in the NFL for the LA Chargers

Three months after attending the two-day speed technique training, Lim's mom, Adrienne (above) sent this email:

Lim asked me to e-mail Phil to let him know that he has gotten his 40-speed time down to a 4.56 already. His coaches are excited. We sincerely thank you for helping us this summer by working him in.

I truly believe that Phil helped him to achieve a goal that he thought he could not reach. To move from running a 5.0 to a 4.56 in such a short time has done wonders for his confidence level. He says that he is going to reach a 4.4 and I believe that he will. Again, thanks for all of your help.
- Adrienne Windham

Coach Phil,

We went on to win the state championship 34-6 and I also won ALL-STATE HONORS at TACKLE. I am now 6'3", 275 lbs, bench 325, p/c-300, squat 450 lbs. I graded out in every game above 80% for an average of 85%. The radio announcer named our O-Line the Mayflower Moving company and named me the Dock Foreman. They say we could move anything. Our offense rushed for almost 4000 yards. I did not give up a sack all year (thanks to quicker feet!).

I was one of 2 seniors on the O-line, with 3 sophomores and 1 junior. I feel like a lot of what you taught me carried over to my leadership skills as well as my performance.

Thanks again man. Your friend, Levi Vedas

Hello Phil,

Thought you might like an update on Addison Quinones. After training with you he continued to use your techniques to work on his speed and the benefits were tremendous. His fastest 40 time was a 4.5 not blinding but quite the increase from where it was. He just finished his freshman year after being recruited by Johns Hopkins University and saw significant time as a defensive back finishing 6th on the team in tackles on their way to capturing their 7th conference title and a final #10 ranking in NCAA D3. He is projected as a starter this coming season. As for high school he was named Defensive Player of the Year in lacrosse, Defensive Player of the Year in football, Overall Player of the Year, Mini-Max Award recipient, 1st Running Back and 2-time first team Defensive Back.

Thank you for your help in making him a better athlete. - Ivan Quinones

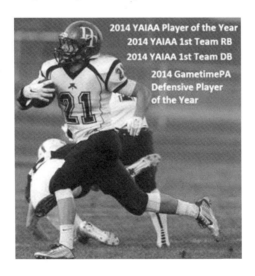

2014 YAIAA Player of the Year
2014 YAIAA 1st Team RB
2014 YAIAA 1st Team DB

2014 GametimePA
Defensive Player
of the Year

I am pleased to pass along some good news about Mitchell. He just returned from the Auburn Jr/Sr Football camp. He had the second fastest 40 time (4.5) at the camp, (out of about 350 participants), for the juniors he had the fastest pro-agility time (4.36) and his vertical jump was 35 inches. All of his times and his jump were much better than last year's camp which were 4.7, 5.1 and 28" vertical jump!! Thank you again for working with Mitchell on such short notice. The techniques you taught him are priceless. - Kim Lewis

Lami Sama, Netherlands sprinter traveling to the US for two days of speed technique training with the focus of staying in drive phase longer

Ray Lewis III working on lateral starting technique by throwing his right elbow knee level one body length away with a crossover step

7

Lateral Speed Technique

While athletes clearly perform more lateral cutting and change-of-direction movements, and very few athletes sprint 20 yards in a straight line, linear speed technique must be taught first and somewhat mastered before lateral speed skill can be successfully introduced.

Once athletes time several linear 20-yard sprints and two flying 20s to begin rewriting suboptimal default running habits with optimal speed technique, adding the lateral speed component only takes a short amount of time. Describing the lateral process and adding it during Speed Technique 101 on the first day is a short 15-minute segment (once linear technique is accomplished).

The reason why it's an easy progressive add is simple. Everything athletes just learned in linear speed technique applies to lateral technique after the first two steps.

The *exercise paradox* kicks in similar to linear speed. Almost every athlete naturally takes a false step rather than the fastest method of a crossover step. Many athletes will take a false step with the back foot and then a quick positioning step with the forward foot. This means the athlete wasted two steps and went nowhere.

I use the pro-agility (5-10-5) shuttle to teach lateral speed. This is a simple drill, but it's great for teaching lateral speed. It is considered a reliable test for agility and used by the NFL Combines and many other sports for testing.

Athletes start from a down position facing forward straddling the start line. They do a lateral start to the right and sprint 5 yards, hand touch the line with the right hand as they are doing a 180-degree change-of-direction turn. They sprint 10 yards to a second 180 turn touching the line with the left hand, and sprint 5 yards past the finish line.

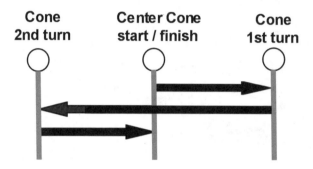

Athletes begin by straddling the center line for this shuttle. While this drill officially begins with a hand down, athletes initially begin upright to learn *lateral speed technique*. The down hand is added later during the timing phase.

Begin by straddling the center line

Next, feet need to be placed in optimal position for lateral movement. When feet are placed side-by-side as shown below, while comfortable, this position naturally forces the body to take a false step.

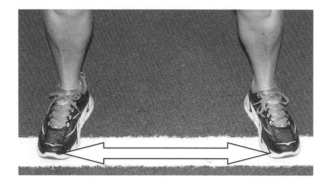

When starting laterally to the right, feet should be aligned toe-to-instep (as Lynn Canelo demonstrates below) so the right hip doesn't block the left leg crossover step. When feet are side-by-side, the right hip blocks the crossover step and forces the crossover step to go wide to the left rather than straight.

The feet side-by-side stance also forces only one leg to push the body forward with a weak one-leg start. Just like the linear start, both legs should push-off equally diving toward the target.

Ever notice how the football quarterback stance has changed in recent years from two feet side-by-side position to a staggered stance? Even in shotgun, pro QBs avoid a side-by-side stance. The reason is simple, two feet side-by-side makes the body want to take a slow and totally wasted false step.

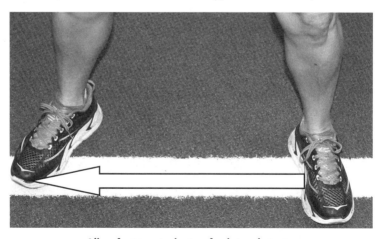

Align feet toe-to-instep for lateral starts

Mistake #1 is athletes performing a lateral start to the right will *step out* with the forward foot (right foot) leading the way. This method is slow because it positions the body too upright, and it doesn't take advantage of gravity and the straight-body forward lean of *drive phase*.

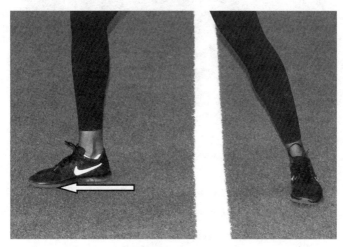

FORWARD STEP is SLOW
Stepping with the right foot for a right lateral start is slow

Mistake #2 is the most common method of beginning a lateral movement because human beings learn to move laterally with the influences of the inner ear that wants us upright and balanced, and the *exercise paradox* of the brain wanting us to perform human movement using slow-muscle fiber in the endurance energy system. These influences make the false-step start natural, but slow.

This mistake is generally called a *false-step start* or a *rocket-step start* because the body actually rocks in the wrong direction to get momentum before moving forward. A *false-step start* is the natural way to perform a lateral start, and it is the slowest method of all. A false-step start (shown right) would be a quick left foot almost moving backward before a quick right foot step. While this movement puts the body pointed in the right direction, athletes have now wasted two steps of time and gone nowhere.

The feet are moving, but the body is in the same place and positioned upright to propel the movement with slow fiber.

It's interesting that the *false-step start* has been tested next to a *forward-step start*. When the two slowest lateral-starting methods are tested, they show the false step is faster. Keep in mind there was no technique training of the fastest way to move laterally. Of course, the natural false step will be faster because this is the default way to move laterally.

No baseball athlete would ever successfully steal a base using the false start or the forward-step start. It takes sprint coaches in track & field hours and hours of focused work over time to get sprinters coming out of blocks forward on the gun and not moving backward into the blocks for the first movement.

The following photo shows what the *false start* looks like AFTER two steps have been wasted. The athlete has gone nowhere. The athlete has taken valuable time to only move and point the body in the right direction.

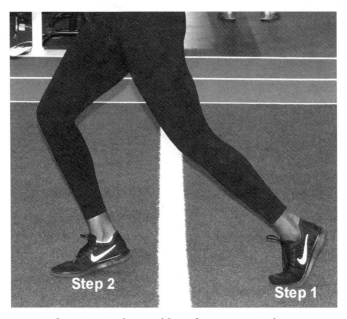

False-step starting position after two wasted steps

The fastest lateral start is using the crossover step. When laterally starting to the right, the back foot (left) crosses over the right leg while simultaneously pushing off with both feet.

Once the crossover step is made, the body is in the position below.

There is one major problem with the crossover start, and there are two solutions. A fast one and a slow one.

Without specialized training, athletes learning the crossover lateral start will naturally use the slowest method because the *exercise paradox* kicks in with the brain trying to propel this start with the leg muscles only with minor movement from the arms. The *exercise paradox* attempts to leave body parts out of the process so there is less muscle to oxygenate.

Athletes are instructed to bring their right hand up into a speed skater stance as shown below by coach Valencia Higgins. Next, they are instructed to throw their elbow hard to the right aiming for *knee level, one body length away*. The elbow traveling incorrectly at chest level is just like *pocket-chest arms* in linear speed. This is how the *exercise paradox* kicks in to make the lateral start slower.

Throw your elbow on go, Set! ... Go! When athletes throw their lead elbow, many make a common mistake unless they have learned a crossover step with the *corrective-arm pump* technique.

Initially throwing the right arm with the first crossover step, athletes end with the left elbow over their left knee as shown (left). Notice that the left arm is over the left knee. This is a huge problem and a huge opportunity to develop the fastest lateral start possible when this issue is corrected the right way.

The left arm over the left knee is NOT how human beings run, walk or sprint. Our limbs move diagonally. The left leg moves with the right arm, and the right leg moves with the left arm.

The first default movement of the crossover step positions us like llamas, camels, bears and giraffes move. They move both legs on one side and then both legs on the other side.

Lateral start BEFORE the corrective-arm pump

The way many baseball athletes who know the crossover step is the fastest lateral start, but don't know the *corrective arm pump* will correct the arms by taking two short baby steps while leaving their arms somewhat out of the process.

Once athletes learn the *corrective-arm pump* to get to the correct position shown below, this will eliminate the need for two baby steps worth of time, and they will cover more distance faster. The *corrective-arm pump* is more strenuous because the heart muscle is having to oxygenate both an upper-body sprint and a lower-body sprint.

Correct lateral start position AFTER the corrective-arm pump

The front view BEFORE the *corrective-arm pump* (left arm over left knee) is shown below, beside the correct lateral start position AFTER performing the quick *corrective-arm pump*.

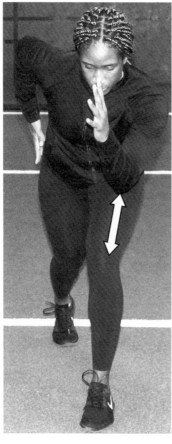 

*Arms position BEFORE
the corrective-arm pump*

*Optimal lateral start AFTER
the corrective-arm pump*

When athletes use their arms for a crossover lateral start with the *corrective-arm pump*, there is more muscle fiber propelling the movement so it's faster, but there's more muscle to oxygenate. Frequently, the *exercise paradox* wins by getting athletes to leave their arms out of the process.

The *exercise paradox* is powerful and it will win out until athletes learn optimal lateral speed technique and practice it *using their arms* during full-speed reps. With practice, correct lateral-speed movements will become the new default as the brain rewrites the old, slow false-step method.

Notice the correct linear starting position below vs. the lateral starting position after the corrective-arm pump has been completed.

LINEAR start second step

LATERAL crossover step with corrective-arm pump

Linear and lateral starts are almost identical after the first two steps. Rather than diving forward into a swimming pool during the linear start, athletes dive laterally with both feet for the first step. Near the end of the lateral crossover step, the corrective-arm pump is made, and at this point, the sprint becomes a linear technique sprint.

Athletes practice a few reps lateral starts with a corrective-arm pump while body positioning and *pocket-chins arms* are checked. Initially, this is like playing the piano and singing at the same time. Some get it in less time than others.

The coaching cue is, *Throw your elbow the direction you want to go, aim knee level one body-length away.* The elbow won't actually travel to knee level, but it will typically travel chest level with the arm too tight to the body just like the *pocket-chest* mistake is made in linear speed technique. It takes a few reps to begin to get the feel for lateral speed technique.

The next step is the instruction to sprint 5 yards using the crossover lateral start with corrective-arm pump and count the number of steps it takes to cover 5 yards.

Most athletes will cover 5 yards laterally in 6 steps when using the false step start. Athletes count their steps. For many, the step count will drop to 4 steps and even 3 steps to cover 5 yards. This immediately makes athletes much faster laterally covering distance in less time. Rather than 6 steps, now it takes 3 steps. The lateral start is performed counting steps for a few 5-yard reps.

Next athletes back up from the start line so they perform side-to-side slides up to the start line where they apply the lateral start from a sliding moving position. Coaches should look for straight body, forward lean, chin down, and throwing the arm knee level rather than chest level with the corrective-arm pump. If athletes lose their balance, this means they are willing to push their inner ear to a new level of speed. Celebrate it! They are getting faster and learning how to make every athletic movement faster.

After athletes experience a few reps and see how their work in lateral speed technique is paying off, the 180-degree change-of-direction technique is added. Athletes are shown *PLOP Position #1*. This includes a hard hip flip before planting their feet for the change-of-direction turn.

Linear and lateral starts are almost identical after the first two steps

Change-of-direction
Plop Position # 1

Anytime an athlete has to do a 180-degree turn, the knees are vulnerable unless a *hip flip* is added where the knees land generally pointed in the direction of the target. There is a slight investment in time to make the hip flip, but by the second step coming out of the 180-degree turn is made, the investment has paid off. It's faster from a performance viewpoint, and the knees are much safer.

Athletes are walked to the 5-yard line, and shown *Plop Position #1,* and asked to get in the position where the hand touches the line. Notice the knees and feet are almost pointed toward the next target. If athletes do the natural default cut, they will land on the line or pass it with knees pointed toward the front, which means the following movement will initially be propelled primarily by the weaker adductors (groin muscles) rather than the strong glutes, hamstrings and calves.

The goal is to not overshoot the 5-yard line. Many athletes will do a two-step overshoot initially -- one wasted step past the line, and one wasted step back.

#1 Agility shuttle change-of-direction hip flip and line touch

Change-of-direction
Plop Position # 2

After athletes practice the speed skater start to Plop Position # 1 for a few reps, they walk 10 yards to the *Plop Position #2* line. They are asked to demonstrate how this change-of-direction maneuver looks with the hip flip and hand down (shown below).

While this exact move is rarely used in sports, it is an embellished change-of-direction move that teaches athletes how to safely cut and change direction from upright sprinting.

#2 Agility shuttle change-of-direction hip flip and line touch

Athletes are given a tip on the way to *Plop position #2*. When they pass the mid-point of the 10-yard piece of the shuttle, and are 4-yards away from another 180-degree change-of-direction turn at *Plop Position #2*, they should be seeing their bodies begin to drop downward toward the line -- otherwise they will overshoot the line with two wasted steps (one step past, and one step back).

Once athletes understand what the correct plop position should look like after the mission-critical hip flip, they practice a couple of reps from the start line. They do the 5-10 section and stop and freeze at *Plop Position #2* with hand on the line so coaches can check the technique.

Athletes now walk to the finish line where it is explained: *It never pays to lunge for the line unless the drill is 5 yards or less.* Since the finish line is 5 yards away from Plop #2, it pays to take a longer last step to hit the line faster.

Once athletes get the feel for the drill, the down start is added. Just as they learned to throw the elbow in the direction they are headed from the speed skater stance, the same occurs with the right hand down and finger tips touching the turf. The down hand carries no weight.

Athletes take a deep breath and with violent ab muscles and even a grunt, they throw their right elbow hard, very hard, *knee level one body length away.* Just like the linear start, athletes should dive to the right pushing off with both feet from a toe-to-instep lateral starting stance. This down start is almost guaranteed to be awkward initially. Like every new speed technique, it pushes the inner ear to a new level of speed it isn't accustomed to yet so the body puts on several braking actions. The arms go to *pocket-chest arms* rather than *pocket-chin arms.* The head pops up, and they may completely lose their balance.

Celebrate fast, out-of-balance starts as this means athletes are pushing their bodies to a new level of speed the inner ear hasn't adapted to yet. But it will, and it only takes about three reps to ease off the inner-ear brakes so athletes can perform lateral technique faster than ever before.

Athletes will see they are almost at the 180-degree turn *Plop Position #1* very quickly. Athletes will see the potential of how applying speed technique will help them perform better in sports.

Athletes are given a mental cue to rehearse before they do this drill. They are advised to recite in their minds several times before starting -- *step step jump, step step jump* because the 5-yard line comes up so fast when athletes push off with both feet diving toward the first target.

It does take practice to refine speed technique for this drill. The pro-agility (5-10-5) shuttle is a kata. It's a dance with precise steps. Applying the science of neuroplasticity to athletic movements, athletes need to practice this drill full speed several times a week until the new technique begins to become the new default.

When optimal speed technique becomes the new default movement for the brain, less reps are required to maintain the technique. Athletes practicing an exaggerated, 180-degree change-of-direction, full-speed cut during the pro-agility shuttle will produce transferable results for other less intense change-of-direction cuts. The impact of shuttle practice on inner-ear brakes is very positive. It's like driving down the freeway 90 MPH, now game speed (70 MPH) will seem slow.

Measurable Performance Improvement

Over the last 40 years, the average improvement I typically see during the first day of Speed Technique 101 is a 2 tenths improvement in the mission critical 20-yard sprint. Athletes aren't stronger yet. The improvement comes simply from learning and applying optimal linear speed technique.

This means the time athletes were sprinting 15 to 16 yards, now they cover 20 yards in the same time. It's noticeably faster for coaches and parents to see, and athletes feel the extra speed.

College biology & chemistry Instructor, exercise science researcher and speed technique specialist, Duane Burt, who is head coach of the MS Elite 2026 (https://www.facebook.com/mselite2026/), uses the speed techniques in this book with softball athletes. He also worked with football coaches at Bogue Chitto High School to conduct an eight-week experiment with this method of teaching linear and lateral speed technique.

Ten high school football athletes trained two days a week. Their performance improvement was remarkable and consistent with what I've seen personally over the years. Football coaches saw an improvement in the pro-agility shuttle of 5.39 tenths. The 20-yard sprint time improved by 2.74 tenths.

Vertical jump improved 2.625 inches. Speed and jumping are close cousins. Good jumpers are usually very fast, and fast sprinters are unusually very good jumpers.

Notice the distance covered with one crossover step when throwing the elbow aiming knee level one body-length away

Lateral start just before the corrective-arm pump

8

Functional Position-Specific Speed

Even though most athletes don't run 20 yards in a straight line very often (other than track athletes), the great majority of time in Speed Technique 101 (the first day) is spent on linear technique. Lateral speed technique is added next in 15 minutes. The mission critical *position-specific speed technique* training comes next. The functional segment (what athletes actually do on the field) can take months to completely master.

Please note, it is a mistake to start at this point in the book and skip the linear and lateral speed technique sections. Everything that happens during functional sports-specific and position-specific speed training is based on athletes learning and practicing linear and lateral speed techniques covered in prior chapters.

Early in my career, I would observe athletes setting records for linear and lateral speed on the turf and track, but when they took their speed skills to the field of play, they went back to default method of moving much slower than their potential.

Transference of speed technique is where the artistry of coaching speed comes into play. Example, I can work with a wide receiver on an out route. The first time this route is run, the athlete plays the old-slow method video game in the brain. The *exercise paradox* and the inner ear influences haven't been overwritten yet for that specific set of movements.

Following are some examples of how to implement sports-specific and position-specific functional speed technique to improve athletic performance.

Football Athletes

I've worked with quite a few receivers over the years including Jerry Rice's son. My speed program was recommended by Raymond Berry, who was the Jerry Rice of his day and made huge catches in the game that put the NFL on the map. I also taught speed technique to two Super Bowl stars, Julian Edelman and Ricardo Lockette.

Frequently receivers start with an upright body and elongated stance. They rock back before going forward and they do the *exercise-paradox* induced false-step start rather than shortening their stance with a straight body and slight forward acceleration lean pushing off with both feet on the QB command. With the typical receiver start, a blitzing linebacker can be at the line of scrimmage before the receiver has actually moved forward because he took two unnecessary steps.

Receivers using the *exercise paradox* default route running method means that he may be the fastest on the team, but the offensive line has to block at least one full second longer because he is rocking backward on the first step.

The second problem that needs to be corrected is receivers frequently run slower to the cut and only sprint after the cut is made. This is the slow default way to run a route, and it adds an additional second to the O-line blocking time.

When speed technique is applied to an out route cutting right, the start is forward on the verbal QB command. The receiver sprints as fast as possible to the cut using acceleration techniques with the Valsalva discussed in Chapter 5 to aggressively accelerate the athlete. The techniques are repeated after the cut giving athletes two acceleration opportunities during this route.

Once receivers get to the functional part of speed technique training where they apply linear and lateral speed technique, they begin to master pass routes much faster. This is a good time to teach athletes that it takes repetitive, quality work on every route in their route tree to begin rewriting the brain with a new, much faster default. After the out-route right gets faster and faster during a few reps, I have receivers to do the out route to the left.

Invariably, the receiver who made significant adjustments to make the out-route right much faster, just ran the out-route left with old, slow default movement. The reason why is explained in an important teaching moment.

The receiver's first attempt to the left is conducted by the brain playing the old-slow video game. Applying speed technique going left is an entirely new video game the brain has yet to learn how to play fast. There is almost zero transference from right to left for the same pass route because the brain has an implanted history of how to do an out-route right and left.

The coaching point is made that speed changes their game in a positive way, but they have to work their route tree, in both directions to overcome old-slow default with every route. Each pass route is its own video game needing to be worked through so speed technique is applied going right and left.

For defensive football athletes, I suggest watching film of Ray Lewis, who may be the GOAT team leader, and who set the example for hard work.

Ray Lewis is always on the list of GOAT linebackers. While he is known for his enthusiasm, leadership and making big plays when needed, Ray Lewis may be the smartest linebacker who ever played the game.

Linebackers are initially taught to take a *read step* equal to the running back's first step. And this is the best way to teach young linebackers when they are first learning football. While a LB read step is the best way to teach young linebackers; from a speed technique standpoint, it's equal to a false-step start that wastes valuable time.

I call these *juvenile mistakes* even though young athletes are just doing what they were taught. When children learn sports at young ages, they aren't strong enough or large enough to perform optimal athletic movements as a mature adult. Young athletes have to compensate and learn many movements in sports the incorrect way just like we first learned to run in upright *fly phase* position because we weren't strong enough to use *drive phase* mechanics.

The linebacker read step is perhaps a *juvenile mistak*e needing to be eliminated as athletes mature. Watch Ray Lewis on film. He figured out the read step wasn't needed. It appears he frequently read the offensive guard's foot movements, eliminated the juvenile read step, and went toward the target faster than others by not wasting time to take the read-step false step.

Commentators said Ray Lewis had great instincts. His instincts came from hard work and deep analytical thinking about how he could know where the play was going by the time most linebackers are finishing their read step.

Defensive back coaches and DB athletes, if you look at *drive phase* body positioning with the forward upper-body lean (shoulders up, back straight, butt down), it's almost identical to the upper-body position during backpedaling. Whether you use the soft-shoe mirroring-the-receiver technique or the kick-step technique in a press stance, if a DB gets too upright, the receiver wins the play.

The kick-step DB technique (Seahawks) is actually a false step, but its purpose is to get the body moving with momentum before a change-of-direction movement and it's made while the DB briefly waits for the receiver to commit.

Offense Guards using a bucket step before pulling is necessary because a crossover step can't be performed fast from an O-line position with teammates on both sides. While optimal lateral speed technique is faster for the pro-agility shuttle and most lateral change-of-direction cuts, it's not best for the bucket-stepping pulling guard who needs to step back before pulling.

Every athletic movement can typically be performed faster by applying the science of neuroplasticity -- perfecting the movement, and practicing it faster and faster with overspeed training.

Football Kickers

Rob Bironas had been released from six NFL teams and was kicking for the New York Dragons in the arena league trying to hang on for one more shot at the NFL. He was accurate but needed distance, and he knew leg speed needed to be increased. In golf, it's club head speed that gets distance. In kicking, it's leg speed.

Before Rob's try out with the Tennessee Titans, I worked with him on speed training strategy. The first recommendation was kick less with more quality. Rob was kicking 50 times a workout. I explained that when he kicked when tired, he was kicking slower and therefore practicing poor technique and training his brain to move slow. This is analogous to trying to run distance to become faster. It does just the opposite.

I recommended cutting back to 25 high quality game-situation kicks per workout. He told me two other kicking coaches told him the same thing.

The second and most important piece was to add the Valsalva breathing, violent abs grunt on every kick to tap into to the way the body is made to go to peak maximal effort that lasts a few seconds. He agreed to add this technique with reducing kicking volume and doing more high-quality reps.

Next we added a posed kicking stance where he would essentially pose for a photo in optimal body positioning with back leg up resting on a box slightly exaggerated for increased hip flexibility. Once set in the optimal position, he would hop forward and kick after a band was placed around his ankle. His leg was pulled approximately 10% faster than it had ever moved before to overspeed optimal kicking technique *(see drill on Soccer Overspeed pages 128-129)*.

The goal with this practice strategy is to improve the nervous system firing by overspeeding optimal kicking technique at a faster rate of speed. This practice helps to remove inner-ear brakes that sneak into most athletic movements.

Rob worked hard for a few weeks before his try out with the Titans. He kicked longer and made the team. He spent nine years with the Titans and went on to set NFL records for the *most game winning field goals in a season* (4 in 2005) and *most points by a kicker in a game* (26 points, October 21, 2007 at Houston Texans). He also set the record for *most consecutive games with a 40+ yard field goal* in NFL history (10).

Rob was selected All-Pro in 2007 and the Pro Bowl in 2008. Like many NFL athletes who were close, but needed just a little speed, Rob worked on speed technique and it paid huge dividends.

As a tribute to Rob's life, I also finish the story by warning athletes to not drink and drive. Rob married Rachel Bradshaw, country music artist and daughter of former NFL Hall of Fame quarterback Terry Bradshaw, who bragged on his wonderful son-in-law on the Tonight Show. Life was good.

One little mistake like not wearing seats belts or drinking and driving can end everything in the blink of an eye.

Sadly, in 2014, around 11 p.m., Rob was killed in a car crash. Toxicology reports showed his blood alcohol level was over the legal limit. As a tribute to Rob, I tell his story to athletes of how hard work as an athlete can pay off, but you can become the best who ever played the game and not enjoy it very long if you drink and drive. Wear your seat belts and don't drink and drive.

In addition to telling athletes about Rob Bironas, I also explain it is never okay to hit a female. While some popular music seems to get away with using derogatory terms for females, it is never acceptable, ever, to hit a female.

No matter how good an athlete is, there is a line that will end a career forever when crossed. Many athletes have spent years working hard to play a game as a profession, only to drop to the bottom the moment they cross the line.

My last warning to athletes I work with is about Jimmy Johns. Not the pizza company, but the high school super star from Brookhaven MS. Jimmy is one of the best athletes I have ever coached. If there were an athlete destined to make it big in NFL, it was Jimmy Johns. He was one of the highest rated QBs coming out of high school after his team won the state championship where he threw 3 TDs and rushed for 107 yards.

Jimmy signed with the University of Alabama and started a few years at RB and set records. A future Heisman Trophy winning RB was his backup.

Jimmy switched to linebacker and was awarded the *Woodrow Lowe Linebacker Award* that is presented to the best linebacker on the University of Alabama football team. He also received the *I Like to Practice Award*.

Coach Saban heard rumors Jimmy was selling drugs and immediately confronted him. Jimmy told me, *If I had not lied to coach Saban, things would have turned out different.* Not long after receiving the *best LB award*, Jimmy was arrested, pleaded guilty and served 13 months in prison for committing a felony, (*https://www.wvtm13.com/article/former-alabama-linebacker-jimmy-johns-brings-football-mentality-to-rest-of-life-after-football-1/3828776*).

While some NFL coaches expressed interest in Jimmy and seeing their potential role of helping an athlete turn his life around, several other NFL athletes were involved in highly-publicized events at the same time for illegal behavior ranging from drugs to domestic violence. There was too much negative publicity focused on NFL coaches, and Jimmy was never given a second chance.

Today, Jimmy Johns is a successful car salesman in southern MS, and he mentors young athletes who have dads in prison.

Like he did making big plays on the field, Jimmy Johns now spends hours every week making *big plays in life* as he mentors young men and teaches them how to stay on the right path.

Quarterbacks

One of the main *position-specific drills* used for QBs is to overspeed the 3- and 5-step pass drops. To set up this drill, the QB does 6 reps of unassisted 3- and 5-step fast drops trying to get to a near *drive phase* lean when headed back to an elbow up, L-throwing position with the ball.

The overspeed trainer bungee cord is attached to the QB's waist. The other end is connected to a stationary object. The QB walks as far away from the cord as it will allow to get it tight. The coach is positioned behind the QB at the midpoint of the stretched bungee, which should be elastic heavy tubing surrounded with a protective sleeve.

From a staggered QB stance, behind center, the QB does a 3-step drop while the coach pulls the QB toward the stationary object with 20-30 pounds of pressure for approximately two seconds. The QB ends each rep in an elbow up, L- throwing position for 3 reps per drop distance. Using the ball makes this drill even more position-specific positive.

The goal is to pull the QB faster with good technique and reprogram the brain and nervous system to move faster for this position-specific movement.

High School QB Matt Bradley 3-step drop with overspeed trainer

QBs do 3 reps of the 3- and 5-step drop from a staggered stance. NOTE: From a speed coach viewpoint, the old two feet side-by-side stance is the slowest possible way to position a QB. Slow and dangerous because the guard can easily step on the QB's foot when he takes the unnecessary false step.

For the starting foot position, you won't find any NFL QBs doing the old side-by-side stance unless you look at old film of Brett Farve. He started out with the old stance early in his career and switched to the staggered speed stance because it's much faster and safer.

To make this drill more position specific, QBs wear helmets when available. With reps, QBs get so much faster on their pass drops. As QBs get faster, the coach pulling the bungee has to literally pull and sprint a few steps to give the athlete an adequate overspeed pull.

Watching film of NFL QBs under center, you will see many lean into a near *drive phase* sprint lean during the drop. The *drive phase* lean forces fast fiber to be recruited to propel the movement, and this makes it faster.

After completing the drop reps, QBs have to fight the *exercise paradox* during the following drill and sprint full speed from the drop to a rollout. First, QBs do a 3-step drop and rollout to the throwing arm side simulating a 10-yard run. Second rep is the rollout to a run with a pull up at the seam for a pass. Last rep, QBs do a classic Russell Wilson rollout toward the seam, pump fake, and do a 180-degree reverse to a run. They do 2 to 3 reps of each drill to the passing arm side first.

The same sprinting reps repeat on the non-throwing arm side next. All together this is 12 position-specific, high-quality sprinting reps and much more productive than running 80% speed sprints at the end of practice during *conditioning*. Football is an anaerobic sport and needs specific anaerobic conditioning.

With this type of structured practice, your QBs practice position-specific, game-like movements that reprogram the brain and nervous system to move faster and faster while anaerobically conditioning the heart muscle specifically for the demands of football.

Every position in football should have a series of drills that replicates exact position-specific movements where anaerobic conditioning can be accomplished during practice when it's fun and athletes can sprint fast.

Coach, important point, this is how the *exercise paradox* works against you and your athletes. If you save the sprinting for the end of practice under the title of *conditioning,* it's just aerobic conditioning that will transfer to the cross-country course, but not the football field.

The benefits athletes get from traditional *conditioning* are based on the number and efficiency of your athlete's mitochondria. And this means the endurance gains from aerobic conditioning will last for around two weeks, and that's it.

If you add position-specific, real-life sprinting during the practice, this will transfer to the field. And it will anaerobically condition your athletes by creating significantly more mitochondria (Chapter 1) that will pay off throughout the game and especially during the 4th quarter.

High School QB Bill Haragree working on drive phase technique

Basketball

When basketball athletes first learn the game, they learn to dribble first, pass and shoot later. When basketball athletes get to the functional sports-specific training section, I ask them to use their speed skill and dribble the length of the court and do a full-speed layup while I count the number of dribbles.

Invariably, they first dribble as they begin to move. They may take 12 plus dribbles to get there and many will do the layup into the bottom of the goal. We walk to the goal and show them speed technique changes their game. Athletes are now getting there so much faster, their layup jump has to be three feet away from the goal. This is very positive once they practice and begin to rewrite the old slow default method.

Once the sports-specific layup is covered, we go back to counting dribbles. I explain; *You covered the court in 12 dribbles, as a speed coach to yourself, think through how you can apply speed technique to get to the layup in less dribbles because every time you dribble you are slowing down and competing with someone who's not dribbling.* Athletes will need less and less dribbles every rep until they get to 5 or 6 dribbles.

If I am working with a basketball team, I'll explain to the coaches in advance they will think I have messed up their shooting and passing ability for a few practices. Players know the speed of their teammates, and they lead passes based on old information about how fast a teammate was before speed technique training.

During the first team practice, almost every pass will be 2 to 3 feet behind the athlete. This is very consistent. It always happens this way, and it's almost humorous to see every pass consistently 2 or 3 feet behind their teammates and many layups frequently hit the underside of the goal. This is positive.

Speed changes the game in a major way. But the first couple of practices, coaches may question this. I explain why this will happen to every coach before beginning, and it only takes a practice or two before the players adapt to the new speed levels and adapt to moving the layup jump point back 3 feet to accommodate much faster athletes.

I had one high school coach during the season tell me his team had a shot at the state championship. He asked if I could help. Once I explained if the play-offs were close and they have a must-win game within two weeks, he would be better off not doing speed technique training. He explained they had two light weeks before the playoffs.

This coach added the speed training including 10 reps of overspeed jumps at the end of every practice. His team won the state championship.

Overspeed jumps are just like the overspeed kicks for Rob Bironas's leg speed work. With basketball athletes, they pair up by equal size and strength. One athlete faces away from the partner and does 10 reps of high-as-possible jumps back-to-back while the partner has hands around the waist of the jumping athlete and attempts to throw the athlete 4 inches higher than ever before during all 10 reps. This drill is demonstrated on pages 121-123.

Athletes are shocked at how hard this drill makes them breathe. This is strength training and cardio because the heart muscle is having to oxygenate all three muscle-fiber types recruited during the jumps.

I am convinced this is the best way to get immediate performance improvement in vertical jump as it helps to pull off the inner-ear brakes.

Baseball & Softball

When it comes to speed, baseball isn't like any other sport with the exception of perhaps the track & field decathlon. Most sports have highly skilled moments to perform. Baseball has a lot more than other sports. Baseball athletes have to sprint, catch, throw, and swing a round bat at a round ball thrown at 100 MPH.

Today, baseball athletes know the game at young ages. They know the smallest details of the game by age 14. If they don't, they may be left behind. I'm not saying this is positive. I'm saying this is the current status of this highly-skilled game. To compete in baseball today, athletes may have a throwing coach, batting coach, and a strength coach just to be on equal standing with others competing for a position on the team. Even with great coaching in all these areas, the number one reason baseball athletes lose out on college scholarship opportunities is lack of speed.

Baseball coaches use the showcase 60-yard sprint to test speed. Like the 40 in football, it's the 60 in baseball. From a linear speed training standpoint, a showcase 60 has three parts. The first 20 yards, *drive phase* rules apply. The second 20 yards, and the last 20-yard segment, *fly phase* rules apply for the last two sections of the showcase 60. The last two segments are identical in technique, except for one part, and that is not stopping before the finish line.

The *exercise paradox* kicks in when athletes stop one to two steps from the finish line. This is a common, a very common, problem for baseball athletes. There is a great opportunity for baseball athletes to improve their 60 time by simply sprinting past the finish line. While athletes in other sports stop before the finish line, this is a huge problem for baseball athletes. I call this the *baseball curse*. No matter what sport I'm working with, when athletes stop sprinting before the finish line, it's called the *baseball curse*.

The reason why baseball gets this title is because baseball athletes have spent years training to slow down to make the turn when rounding first base. In essence, baseball athletes have trained themselves to stop before the finish. When you add the *exercise paradox* to the constant practicing of slow-down-before-the-finish sprinting, this practice doesn't disappear when timing the Showcase 60. *Baseball curse* is not an easy habit to break.

Coaching your athletes to *run through* will not work. Athletes telling themselves to *run though* will not work. To become successful at not stopping before the 60-yard finish line, athletes must quite literally fake their brain off and visualize the finish line 3 to 5 yards past the actual finish line.

I've had baseball athletes headed to Harvard, Yale, Dartmouth and Stanford who have 4.0 GPAs and are very bright, but they have problems with the *baseball curse* finish.

The *exercise paradox*, inner-ear brakes, and the years of practicing to slow down before the finish line are very powerful video games in the brain of baseball athletes. The *run through* advice will not overcome this problem without focused practices.

Here's what coaches can look for to know when athletes are stopping too soon. Listen to their footsteps. You will hear consistent sounds when sprinting fast and striking the surface mid foot. When you hear a soft step or a loud flat step, this means the athlete quit sprinting one step before you heard it.

After 40 years of working on the *baseball curse* with some really bright athletes, I can tell you the *run through* coaching strategy doesn't work. Athletes have to fake the brain off by visualizing the finish line being past the real finish line and practice it for weeks prior to the showcase. Fixing this one piece can easily be worth a 2 tenths faster 60.

I haven't worked a lot of college baseball teams, but the ones I've worked with get an average improvement in the showcase 60 of a full half second. Two tenths of it is in addressing the *baseball curse*. The other three tenths, come from correcting *drive phase* and *fly phase* technique.

Mastering the crossover step with corrective-arm pump can also produce a 1- to 1.5-tenths improvement when starting laterally. Hitting the acceleration point coming out of the ladder (Chapter 4) can yield another tenth. Hitting the next two acceleration points in the 60 can yield another tenth (Chapter 6).

Like other sports, baseball athletes can get 2 tenths faster from linear technique training in the 20-yard sprint, but when they go to the field for functional movements, the brain will go back and play the old, slow video game because default performance hasn't been fully reprogrammed with new faster technique specifically for baseball movements.

The following information shows how linear and lateral speed technique can be transferred to functional, on-the-field, common baseball movements.

Using the *drive phase* acceleration ladder aimed at first base, the baseball / softball athlete stands at the plate facing a simulated pitcher. The athlete swings, drops the bat safely, and sprints through the ladder toward first base using their new *drive phase* speed skill for two acceleration points.

Starting position
bat up
safe swing
drop bat safely
sprint through
acceleration ladder
demonstrated by
coach Joe Bala, MSE
Exercise Science
(www.bulletfitllc.com)

During the first two steps, coaches will see the *exercise paradox* kick in as the brain attempts to play a new faster video game. Athletes who did this perfectly earlier with the body dropping into *drive phase* and slowly coming up (like an airplane taking off) will go back to running high until they work through a few reps applying speed technique after swinging the bat.

Swing and safely drop bat

Drop body into Drive Phase position and sprint through acceleration ladder with Pocket-Chin Arms

It will take a few reps to begin rewriting default with new and faster linear speed technique. The next time the athlete runs bases, the difference in speed will be noticeable by coaches, parents, and the athlete will know his speed work is paying off and want more reps to keep improving.

While recording performance (one page per athlete), one of the great things about this speed technique training system, you don't have to pull a piece of paper out and convince athletes they are improving. They do see it on paper, but they physically feel their new level of speed.

Should you not have an indoor training facility and can't get a field when student athletes need to practice, the Matrix S-Drive is a great speed technique training tool. I have been a consultant for the parent company, Johnson Health Tech (Cottage Grove, Wisconsin) for over 15 years, and I was involved in the refinement of the S-Drive (for *drive phase* sprinting). I wrote the speed technique training protocols for coaches that can be downloaded from this book's website.

The exact same baseball / softball drill, simulated swing, safely drop bat and sprint to first can be performed on the Matrix S-Drive self-propelled treadmill. The S-Drive is perfect for cold-weather and hot-weather environments.

The athlete stands on the metal platform as shown by coach Joe Bala in the Edge Performance Center, ClubSport San Jose (*www.clubsportfit.com*). The baseball / softball athlete swings the bat safely or simulates swinging the bat, and drops the body into *drive phase* technique for the drive-up drill, which is 5 full-speed sprint steps with hands on the lowest rung. Without slowing down, hands move up to the next bar for 5 full-speed steps, then to the next bar up for 5 sprinting steps, then to the top bar for 5 sprinting steps.

This drill trains athletes to drop the body into *drive phase* positioning after swinging the bat for a high-quality sprint to first base. The body should come up like an airplane taking off -- straight body coming up slow while legs and arms pump full speed.

Batting stance standing on rails, simulated swing, drop bat, sprint to first with the Matrix S-Drive Drive-up drill

Perfect for cold-weather and warm-weather environments, Matrix S-Drive was made for indoor drive phase and fly phase speed training for sprinting sports like baseball, softball, football, track, basketball, soccer, lacrosse and rugby

Quite by accident, one day while working with university baseball team athletes during Speed Technique 102 (day two of training with focus on sports-specific functional speed technique application), one athlete ran a 20-yard sprint for time using his glove while applying *pocket-chin arms* taught in linear Speed Technique 101 the first day.

The athlete kept the glove away from his body. His time was fast. When I saw his time compared to his other times, this athlete ran faster with the glove than without.

I was shocked at his performance and asked a few other athletes to time with their gloves. Initially, this was difficult for them not to run with the glove tight to their chests with the slower *pocket-chest* mechanics (shown below). The *exercise paradox* and the inner ear will put on speed brakes by unconsciously pulling the arms (including the arm with the glove) close to the chest.

Incorrect speed technique sprinting with the glove.
Body too upright and glove too tight to the chest

Once the athletes worked through a few reps with the glove attempting to keep the glove in *pocket-chin arms* technique with the glove away from the body, every athlete ran faster with the glove. I'm still amazed at how this works to help athletes cover more ground faster. But it works for every baseball athlete I've worked with over the years.

The challenge for coaches and athletes is this technique takes practice because it is very difficult to keep the glove away from the body. Baseball athletes have learned to sprint with a glove almost touching the chest for years, and it takes time to rewrite the old-slow default method of sprinting with a glove.

Correct speed technique sprinting with the glove.
Body straight, forward lean. Arm mechanics are
pocket-chin with the glove away from the body

When baseball athletes first try this speed technique with the glove, it will feel awkward because it is totally different than the default method. Typically, it takes 3 reps of practicing a new technique just to get the brain out of the awkward mode.

Speed technique with a glove applies to softball athletes. Glove too tight to the chest results in incorrect speed technique demonstrated by softball coach, Mina E Garcia (instagram.com/minaflexmuscle/)

Getting the glove away from the body with pocket-chin technique during sprinting to the ball will lengthen stride and athletes will cover more ground with every step

Sprinting with a glove can also be performed on bad weather days with the Matrix S-Drive by getting the glove away from the body as shown below by coach Joe Bala. The S-Drive belt is attached before this drill begins and athletes simply sprint into the belt using *fly phase* technique with the glove.

While positive for all baseball athletes who sprint with a glove, this drill is especially effective for outfielders.

An additional way to use the Matrix S-Drive with baseball athletes is a unique sprinting rep that I learned from Dan Richter (*https://www.facebook.com/dan.richter.1671*). Since Dan created this innovative rep that places the body into an exaggerated low, *drive phase* position for sprinting and sled pushing work, I call this the *Richter Rep* in the S-Drive Protocols.

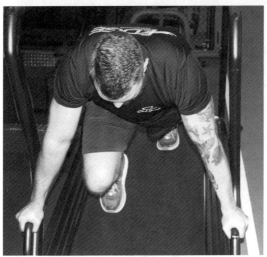

Richter Rep on the Matrix S-Drive

Overspeed Jumps

Since softball and baseball athletes frequently need to jump high to make a catch, adding 10 reps of *overspeed jumps* at the end of practice will quickly improve their vertical jumping performance.

When athletes train legs hoping this will help them run faster and jump higher, they are frequently disappointed. Here's why. Because their legs are getting stronger, when they jump vertically, the inner-ear slams on the brakes and the calves, plantars and other muscles that propel jumping high deactivate so the athlete won't fall. The brain senses the extra leg strength and sends messages to the brain to put on the brakes.

Overspeed jumps remove the inner-ear brakes. Doing this drill, you can see this process occurring during the first set. Athletes pair up in equal size for this drill that last 3 minutes. The starting *ready position* is shown below.

The jumping athlete does 10 non-stop, rapid-fire jumps trying to jump as high as possible on every rep. The assisting athlete (or coach) throws the athlete 4 to 6 inches higher than the athlete has jumped before on every rep.

During the first reps, coaches can see the inner-ear working to adapt to a new jumping height. When the athlete comes down for the first two reps, athletes will briefly struggle for balance because the inner-ear isn't accustomed to jumping that high, which means the brakes are still on.

After those first reps, coaches will see athletes jumping higher and higher and gaining balance as they land. This means the inner-ear is relaxing at the new height and releasing the brakes. Softball coach, Mina E. Garcia (*Instagram.com/minaflexmuscle/*) and coach Joe Bala demonstrate overspeed jumps.

I recommend doing this drill without a glove the first couple of times. After athletes are jumping higher and landing balanced, add the glove for the last 5 reps for a more sports-specific functional exercise.

Overspeed jumps remove inner-ear braking for increased jump height

Soccer

When children in soccer first learn how to run and kick the ball, they typically run to the ball and dance a few shuffle steps to position the body before kicking. They have to do this as children. This is slow speed technique, but it's absolutely necessary for children to learn this way.

As soccer athletes mature, they need to eliminate the pre-kick shuffle dancing, unless they are setting up a diversion for a defender.

As a speed coach, I see the slow-down shuffle dance even with college soccer athletes. They don't need the shuffle dance before they kick, but it's an imprinted default in the brain as a carry-over from how they first learned to play. Coaches can help athletes remove the unnecessary pre-kick shuffle, but it takes practice. The following speed drill will help to accomplish this objective.

Functional speed technique training for soccer begins with a tap pass in front of the acceleration ladder before hitting *drive phase* acceleration positioning (shown right). The athlete is moving from an upright position during the pass to a hard drop into an acceleration forward lean with *pocket-chin arms*. Initially, the tap pass-to-sprint rep will feel foreign during the first reps as the upright false-step start seems to impact soccer athletes the first few reps.

Once the sprint begins to become more like *drive phase* than upright *fly phase*, the much slower *pocket-chest arms* (that plagues soccer athletes) needs to be addressed. I'll frequently pull out a couple of 8X10 photos of Lionel Messi and Kylian Mbappe sprinting to show how they use their arms violently with *pocket-chin arms* speed technique to propel sprinting bursts during a game.

It takes several practice reps to get the inner ear to release the brakes for soccer athletes who have practiced and played in *fly phase* technique for years. Once they begin to master *drive phase* technique functionally with a ball, it is amazing how much faster soccer athletes become.

The next rep also begins with a tap pass in front of the ladder followed by sprinting through the ladder and adding *acceleration point 2* (coming out of the ladder) for a full 20-yard sprint. Sprinting a lot faster means the slow-down distance after the sprint is a lot longer. The longer slow down proves a point to soccer athletes as they see themselves covering most of a soccer field when applying only two acceleration techniques.

The teaching point; *look how far you just ran when you used two acceleration techniques. You just about covered the whole field. In your next practice, try two acceleration techniques during one sprint burst and see how far and fast this will take you.*

Josephine Cotto, 8th grade soccer athlete demonstrates the tap pass-to-sprint drill at the Riekes Center, Menlo Park CA. Two years later at age 15, she competed in World Cup Qualifiers for the U17 and U20 Puerto Rican National team

When I'm working with a soccer team for two speed technique sessions (101 & 102), I'll set up my favorite soccer speed technique drill. One acceleration ladder goes near the sideline for half of the team in Group 1 (shown below). The second acceleration ladder goes in the center of the field past the mid-field line so athletes see they can be past the midfield line and still be in a play *when they make the effort* to execute two acceleration techniques.

Soccer Team Speed Technique Drill

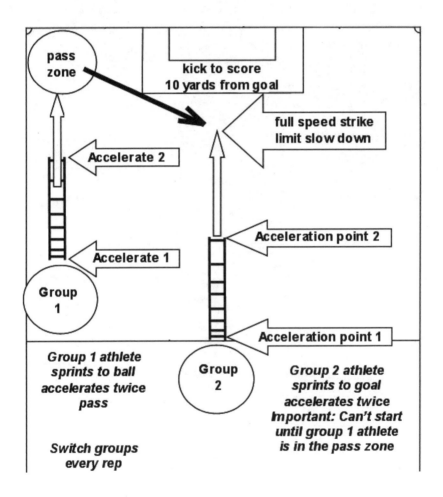

There are two athletes in each play, but the Group 2 athlete can't leave early. Group 2 athlete must wait until the Group 1 athlete sprints through the ladder, accelerates twice to enter the kick pass zone where a ball is waiting. Now the Group 2 athlete can start. Group 1 athlete doesn't wait to kick.

Group 1 athletes kick pass should be immediate and will be different than normal play in that the ball should be aimed 10 to 15 yards in front of the goal for the Group 2 athlete to sprint to the ball and take a shot 15 yards out *without slowing down*.

One goal of this drill is to teach athletes that two acceleration techniques in one sprint can cover more than half the field amazingly fast. Another goal is to get athletes to remove the pre-kick shuffle dance. They are instructed to kick and score and don't worry where the ball is going. Aim at the goal but kick hard *without slowing down*.

Soccer coaches are amazed during the first couple of reps, almost no one hits the goal. The ball goes wide, really wide, because the *exercise paradox* and the inner ear are still trying to control their movements. But they're beginning to rewrite default with much faster speeds.

After a few reps, magic happens. The ball starts to hit the net with much more power than the athletes have experienced before. The velocity of the sprint before a kick adds to the velocity of the leg speed during the kick. This is similar to a javelin thrower's run up before the throw. It adds velocity.

While accuracy is sacrificed for a few reps, the brain quickly adapts to the new movement at a much faster level of speed. In one 2-hour speed technique session, the whole team will be much faster linearly, laterally, and most important, functionally for the game of soccer.

I can teach athletes how to run much faster linearly and laterally, but they don't take it to the field unless they make the transference with functional speed technique application for several full-speed reps of every soccer movement they perform. This is the best drill I've seen to help athletes take speed technique improvements to the field.

This drill does something else that's magical too. If the drill is performed after warm-up and before practice, athletes will practice significantly faster after the drill. The best analogy for this is the example of driving on the freeway 70 MPH on a long trip and pulling off to get gas. Here, 50 MPH feels like you are crawling because your brain is accustomed to the higher rate of speed.

The end result of using this drill is obvious. When athletes practice faster, they recruit more fast IIa and IIx muscle fiber and create micro-trauma in all three fiber types so when they sleep, the muscle fiber heals back bigger and stronger. This means athletes practicing speed technique will keep getting faster and faster.

Since the heart muscle is oxygenating a lot more muscle fiber, athletes are conditioning the anaerobic process, as well as the aerobic process of the heart muscle. Plus, they get the added benefit of mitochondria growth, which is the source of endurance at the cellular level.

During Speed Technique 102 on the second day, the kicking overspeed drill (below) is added for *soccer athletes* just like it would be with football field goal kickers and *rugby athletes*. One at a time, an athlete poses with the kicking knee back slightly exaggerated for hip flexibility improvement with a band around the ankle as shown below by soccer athlete and strength coach Eric Allen at ClubSport San Jose (*eallen@clubsportfit.com*).

From the starting position, the athlete hops forward with the front leg and swings the back-kicking leg through simulating a long kick. The coach is on the other end of the short bungee cord.

With a tight cord, and after the hop forward, the coach pulls the leg slightly faster than it's moved before with good technique and safe follow through. The goal is to pull the slightly exaggerated, kicking leg through the kick while assisting the brain and nervous system to move 10% faster. In essence, the athlete is reprogramming his brain and nervous system to move faster while getting rid of the *exercise paradox* and the inner-ear brakes during kicking movements.

Overspeed kicking movements reprogram the brain and nervous system to fire faster for soccer, football place kickers, and rugby athletes. Before every rep, the athlete should be balanced and ready. The athlete hops forward (as shown) simulating the kicking movement while the coach pulls the kicking leg faster for 3- to 5-reps per leg.

Lacrosse

Applying linear and lateral speed technique that lacrosse athletes learn during Speed Technique 101 on day one is complex because there is an implement involved, a short stick for attack and a long stick for defense.

While the principles of *drive phase* and *fly phase* technique apply, it takes practicing with the lacrosse stick to master the forward lean and *pocket-chin arms*. I can coach athletes to sprint much faster linearly and laterally, but the moment they pick up their stick for functional speed training (with the stick and gear), the brain takes them back to default method of running upright with the stick too close to the chest.

The way the functional component is added is the *turn and sprint drill* with the stick. Once athletes are comfortable using speed technique with their stick, the ball is added for the *catch and sprint drill* with the ball to simulate game conditions.

The athlete will catch the ball or scoop it from the ground and sprint through the ladder hitting two acceleration points, one at the start and one coming out of the ladder. After 20 yards, the attack short stick athletes get to add a shot at the 20-yard point. When lacrosse athletes sprint full speed with the ball, the stick needs very little wrist cradling to keep the ball in the basket. Centrifugal force will keep the ball in the basket once the athlete begins to sprint fast.

To make it more specific, a second drill is added for attack players. They will catch the ball 5 yards behind the goal, sprint in a wide circle to the front of the goal 10- to 15-yards away to make a shot.

Female lacrosse sticks being smaller means two hands on the short and long stick when they have the ball. Male attack players with practice can learn to sprint with the stick cradling the ball in one hand for additional speed before making a shot or passing.

Matt Linton demonstrates drive phase speed technique
using pocket-chin arms with the lacrosse defensive long stick

Overspeed Training for Linear Speed

Overspeed training via elastic-cord assistance is referred to as *supramaximal* because athletes will be sprinting faster than they can run without assistance. Overspeed training is proven in research to improve the sprinting speed of athletes. Researchers Corn and Knudson report:

> *Elastic-cord tow training resulted in significant acute changes in sprint kinematics **in the acceleration phase**,*
> (Corn, R.J. (2003) *Effect of elastic-cord towing on the kinematics of the acceleration phase of sprinting.* J. Strength Cond Res 17, pp.72–75).

In a study reviewing the research on resisted and assisted (overspeed) training, researchers Leyva, Wong, and Brown conclude:

> *Coaches and athletes wanting to acutely reduce ground contact time, increase stride length and frequency **should use overspeed training**,*
> (Leyva WD, Wong MA, Brown LE (2017) *Resisted and Assisted Training for Sprint Speed: A Brief Review.* J Phy Fit Treatment & Sports: 555554).

Important point for overspeed training, it must be performed with optimal technique. Overspeed reps with poor technique defeats the purpose. The goal is to play the optimal linear speed technique video game in the brain, but moving 10% faster than the athlete can sprint without the assistance of the bungee-cord tow.

While *resisted sprinting* with weighted vests and parachutes can be effective in building strength, and this modality certainly has a role in an on-going speed improvement program, there is an issue that needs discussion.

A deep dive into the research concerning overspeed vs. resisted training can present misleading results. Here's why. The research shows overspeed is more effective from the start up to 15 yards, and resisted training may have a slight advantage at 15 to 30 yards. The problem is overspeed is a 15-yard assisted sprint and there isn't a reliable way to pull an athlete more than 15 yards.

I can't tell you how many times parents flying athletes for speed technique training have told me, *my son has been going to a performance center for a year, and he looks like he should be faster, but he isn't. I think there is a technique problem and this is why we are here.*

Athletes attending the two-day Speed Technique camps will significantly improve their 20-yard sprint times once they learn optimal technique. However, this isn't true performance improvement until it transfers to functional position-specific movements on the field.

Overspeed position-specific reprogramming drills get the job done, but this is where it becomes challenging for coaches.

Coaches in sprinting sports like football, softball, baseball, soccer, lacrosse, basketball and rugby, functional drills require creativity to structure drills that practice exact position-specific movements with optimal technique faster than game speed.

Several overspeed drills have been described in this chapter, but the best drills have yet to be created. Coach, you have a great opportunity to take the information in this book and build on it for every position on your team.

The history of overspeed training began with Dr. George Dintiman in the 1960s. He pulled athletes behind cars to force them to sprint fast with longer strides. He reports improvements in speed as much as 6 tenths in a 40-yard sprint during 8 to 12 weeks of overspeed training, (Dintiman, G. Ward, B. Tellez, T. (1997) *Sports Speed Second Edition*, Champaign, IL. Human Kinetics p. 193*).

For linear overspeed training, the best program for *fly phase* speed development is the Athletic Republic high-speed treadmill (that will clock 30 mph) and their protocols developed by John Frappier (*www.athleticrepublic.com*) and refined by Dr. Steve Swanson, Founder and CEO at Treadmetrix; AccuPower Solutions (*www.treadmetrix.com*).

Charlie Graves, a former Olympic-level swimmer and professional triathlete is the CEO of Athletic Republic and has locations across the U.S. with professionally-designed off-season programs for many different sports. The coaches at Athletic Republic have gone through rigorous training and testing before being certified. While Athletic Republic facilities may be different sizes in different locations, the high-quality standardized programming for various sports is superb.

Without high-speed treadmill availability, linear overspeed can be accomplished on the field by using a *doubleman overspeed trainer*, which is elastic heavy tubing surrounded with a protective sleeve 20-feet long and stretches to 55 feet. It is used differently than the package recommends however. One end of the bungee cord is connected to a stationary goal post or fence.

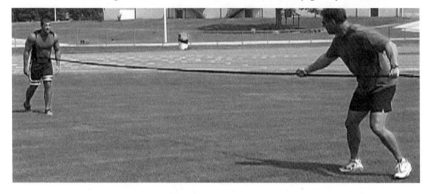

The other end of the bungee is attached to the athlete's waist belt. The athlete walks until the cord is fully stretched, and turns 180 degrees to face the coach. The coach is positioned at the midpoint of the stretched bungee (shown above with Adam November).

The speed coach (or experienced teammate) has both hands on the cord preparing to pull the athlete 10% faster than the athlete has ever sprinted before for 15 - 20 yards. The athlete sprints to the finish line where the cord is attached. Essentially, the coach or pulling athlete will be in a simulated lane one and the sprinting athlete will be in lane two. Explain this so you don't get run over. The coach will be pulling approximately 20 to 30 pounds of pressure for adult athletes, much less for younger athletes.

With the bungee fully stretched, and you see the athlete focused and ready to sprint, the coach says, *ready, set, GO* and begins to pull slightly before the *GO* command.

With a team or small group, once athletes see the first rep, they understand the mechanics and the purpose of this overspeed drill

Athletes are instructed to *attempt to out run the tension in the cord, and don't slow down until they cross the finish line* (where the bungee cord is anchored). Athletes will be traveling at a much faster speed and need to be aware of the limited room to slow-down and stop (the length of the bungee cord).

When pulling the bungee cord, the overspeed sprint lasts 3 to 4 seconds. Once the athlete is sprinting beside the coach, the coach or athlete doing the pulling, raises the bungee high overhead so it doesn't go between the legs of the sprinting athlete.

Some sprinting athletes may grab the bungee, but they need the arms free to work *pocket-chin arms* at a high rate of speed.

Two methods come into play. As the speed coach, you can have athletes turnaround and get set to sprint back for two back-to-back reps, or you can have the athlete walk back to the original starting point. Normally athletes do two reps. I've tested up to five reps, and at this point in the technique training, more than two reps is generally too much. However, if this is part of a speed workout, 4 reps can be performed with good technique.

What happens during this drill is the brain senses athletes are taking their full-body weight and propelling it 20 yards, much faster than ever before, and the heart muscle kicks into anaerobic performance mode with a high heart rate. Around 5 reps, many athletes will actually get dizzy from the abnormally high heart rate. In 30 years of pulling athletes with the overspeed trainer, I've never gone past 5 reps with an athlete. The standard practice is 2 reps of overspeed on day one, and 2 to 4 reps on day two.

While this is a great cardio exercise for creating more ATP-producing mitochondria that significantly increases endurance capacity, the moment a speed drill begins to repeat with poor technique, this is in essence, training athletes to run slow. It's wise to stop when optimal technique fails.

Another way to perform overspeed technique training is to run slightly downhill. But hold on. Downhill running has an important caveat needing consideration. Dintinman, Ward and Tellez, recommend in their book that the slope decline needs to be 1- to 3.5-degrees and not more, (*Sports Speed.* Second Edition. 1997, p193*)*. More than a 3.5-degree slope makes athletes sprint with poor foot-striking technique, which defeats the purpose of the drill.

Football fields typically have a 1- to 1.5-degree slope from the crown to the sidelines for rain drain requirements. While not ideal for overspeed training, it's adequate when athletes sprint diagonally from the center of the 50-yard line to an end-zone pylon. This method is a good backup when the bungee overspeed trainer isn't available or you have a large team and limited time.

Soccer athlete Noe Guzman, Silver Creek Sportsplex,
Sports Manager doing overspeed sprinting with coach Marc Kondo
pulling the overspeed bungee cord to remove inner-ear brakes and
reprogram the brain and nervous system to move faster

Noe Guzman at the Silver Creek SportsPlex San Jose (https://gotoplex.com) doing the functional speed technique application drill for soccer, tap pass and sprint in the acceleration ladder with a coach checking for forward lean, straight body, and pocket-chin arms

Jerry Rice Jr. working on lateral starting technique with the pro agility (5-10-5) shuttle

9

Speed Abs

Speed Abs workout doesn't mean to do heavy crunches as fast as possible. *Speed Abs* is a quick program for significantly strengthening the abdominal muscles of athletes so they will have extra strength to violently tighten abs to take the body to peak maximal strength during acceleration bursts.

Without question, I know that this approach of training abs will raise the eyebrows of many coaches, parents and athletes. The *Speed Abs* method of training will initially sound totally contradictory to what many have been taught over the years. However, let me challenge you to do two things: Read the entire chapter with an open mind, and simply test drive this method for yourself. It only takes five minutes. Fair enough?

I'm old, but not old school. In the 1990s, when I wrote my first book to motivate adults, not just athletes, but adults of all ages to use fast-fiber, anaerobic sprint-cardio training that targets exercise-induced growth hormone, long-slow cardio was king during that time, and it had been king for years.

I was questioned about my thinking and training methods for years, laughed at by some, but I was totally vindicated on August 8, 2007 when the American Heart Association and the American College of Sports Medicine changed the cardio guidelines by essentially dropping long-slow, low-intensity cardio (because the research shows this does not get results). They added two new guidelines for cardio: 30 minutes of moderate intensity cardio 5 days a week, or vigorous intensity cardio 20 minutes 3 days a week.

The new high-intensity cardio guideline matched the *Sprint 8 Cardio Protocol* recommendation in my book written a decade earlier, specifically, 20-minutes of high-intensity cardio training 3 days a week.

The protocol is composed of 8 anaerobic, fast-fiber recruiting, 30-second sprint bursts on a traditional gym cardio unit followed by 90 seconds of active recovery. Sprint 8 can be accomplished by sprint running, sprint swimming or cardio sprinting on a cardio machine. For the past 15 years, Sprint 8 has been the featured sprint cardio program on award-winning cardio machines made by Matrix Fitness. While HIIT is vogue today, in the 1990s, people thought I was crazy, so I'm no stranger to controversy. And *Speed Abs* is in that category.

When it comes to training abs, there are many prevailing views just as there were about long-slow cardio in the 1990s. This is why I ask every reader to put this method to a personal test before passing judgment.

Speed Abs was created to make ab muscles much stronger so they can help to pull the body forward during short sprints and help to take the body to peak max effort with the Valsalva technique during strategic accelerations points.

It was erroneously taught in the 90s that those who wanted to achieve spot reduction around the waistline should do high-rep training because it was generally believed that high reps made an area of the body smaller, and low reps would make the waist line larger. We laugh at this thinking today when it comes to overall strength training, yet many coaches and personal trainers still teach their clients to do a lot of high reps when it comes to training abs.

Today, we know that the body adapts to the micro-fiber tears in the muscle worked during training by healing and remodeling during sleep and recovery over a 24- to 48-hour period.

Counting the number of reps, amount of resistance, and measuring the velocity of movement of the exercise selected when strength training are tools of the trade. But it's important to understand that the body heals the micro-fiber tears caused during training and this is what builds and strengthens muscle.

This is why we train muscles in the body in the first place. And this is why we train the heart muscle. The goal is to create micro-trauma in the muscles to start the adaptation process so these muscles will adapt by becoming bigger and stronger.

With this in mind, let me ask a question: Why do most people continue to recommend high reps for training abs? Could this be carryover thinking from some very old ideas that high reps can make the waistline smaller? Probably.

Another question, what would you get out of 100 reps of bench press? Here's the answer. The weight would have to be so light to get 100 reps; the joints may get too much trauma, and the muscles may get tired. But this low-intensity exercise will not create a lot of muscle trauma that builds muscle during sleep.

An athlete can work chest, shoulders and triceps muscles with 100 reps on bench press, but think of the wear and tear on the shoulder joints and elbows. When athletes only train slow-muscle fiber with light resistance, the only way to get progressive overload is to do more and more reps that take longer and longer.

You can train the heart muscle with moderate-intensity cardio, but this method takes 30 minutes 5 days a week, or you can deploy a high-intensity Sprint 8 cardio training strategy and accomplish more in 20 minutes 3 days a week (of which only 4 minutes is hard cardio sprinting on a cardio unit). The same thinking needs to be applied when training abs.

Why wear-out the spine with high-rep ab training and waste all that time when there is a much better way to get the job done.

Physiology and Efficiency of Ab Muscles

Think about how ab muscles are positioned on the human body. Ab muscles are used almost constantly during waking hours, and ab muscles are in rows for an important reason. The separate rows of abs make this muscle group one of the most efficient muscle groups in the entire body, perhaps second to the human heart that can beat without missing or taking a break for over 100 years.

Visualize how the different rows of ab muscles work in slow motion when doing a sit up. When the top row of abs engages and contracts to start to move the upper body upward, the other rows of abs are somewhat relaxed.

As the upper body continues to rise, the second row engages and the top row begins to relax with the other rows. The third row then engages, and then the top two rows begin to relax. The rows of ab muscles are a wonderful display of the efficiency of the human body as they work in tandem to endure all day.

Ab muscles are able to contract and relax to propel movement consistently for a lifetime. We may wear out the spine, but the ab muscles just keep on going. Working together as a unit, ab muscles are so efficient, they seem to endure forever.

While TV advertisements often show thermogenic images of all the ab muscles working together on the latest fad exercise device, this is not how the ab muscles are made to work, nor is it the best way to train your abs.

There's a better way to get the abs muscles significantly stronger in just a couple of weeks. Doing 1000 reps and taking 20 to 30 minutes of precious training time with athletes is not near as effective as training abs heavy. Here's how to do *Speed Abs.*

Start with a 25 to 35-pound plate on the floor for a heavy crunch. The low back stays in contact with the floor. The goal is to select a weight that's so heavy the athlete thinks 10 reps will be difficult. But they can always do 20 reps. I give the same instruction to 75-year old adults, but using 10 pounds to start.

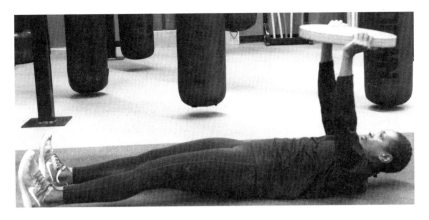

Every rep has to be a very heavy crunch. The instruction to athletes is *it has to be so heavy 10 reps will be very hard, but hang on for 20 reps.*

Athletes should expand the rib cage fully during the starting point of every rep. This is an important step to eliminate the e*xercise paradox* impact of trying to make this exercise less intense (by recruiting less muscle fiber). The body will not want to naturally expand the rib cage to make the exercise easier.

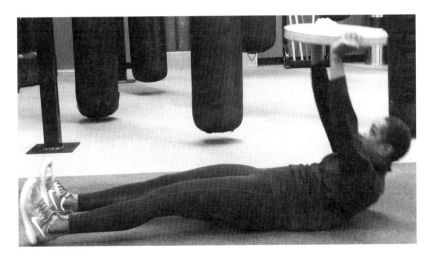

Athletes start with two sets and slowly build to four sets of heavy crunches. Based on time, two sets of heavy *Speed Abs* can be very effective.

Important point: Once the upper ab muscles are exhausted from the heavy crunches, they will be in a weaken state and can't synergistically assist the lower abs to raise the legs, which is the way *Speed Abs* is finished.

Immediately after the last set of heavy crunches, and *without resting*, begin two sets of 20 reps of some type of leg raises. Athletes will quickly notice the effort to raise the legs is much more difficult. This is because their upper ab muscles are exhausted and aren't able to assist when raising the legs.

Leg Raises demonstrated by coach Valencia Higgins

Recovery should be 30 seconds. Athletes should feel like they have been to a 30-minute abs class -- only difference is they have only done 60 reps to 120 reps in less than 5 minutes.

Advanced versions of *Speed Abs* can be done on a Bosu stability ball with heavy dumbbells. An advanced version is demonstrated below by retired NFL Tight End, Mikhael Ricks, an outstanding performance coach and speed coach specialist in Miami Florida, (*http://mikhaelricks.com*). Mikhael was drafted in the 2nd round. He played for the San Diego Chargers, Kansas City Chiefs, and the Detroit Lions where he was a Pro Bowl selection.

An advanced version of leg raises is shown by Mikhael Ricks below. Another version of *Speed Abs* can be one set heavy crunches followed immediately by a 20-rep set of leg raises (for two to four sets).

The *Speed Abs* program was created to help athletes get significantly stronger abs to help pull them forward in *drive phase*. The side effect of *Speed Abs*, the 60- to 120-rep program, really works the abdominal muscles for adults of all ages in 5 minutes.

Advanced version of Leg Raises demonstrated by performance coach Mikhael Ricks, NFL Tight End (1998–2004) http://mikhaelricks.com

Another advanced version of Speed Abs is on a bench press bench. Going heavy with 185 pounds X 20 crunches is two-times Super Bowl championship, Super Bowl MVP, and GOAT middle linebacker, Ray Lewis. It was an honor to work with three of Ray's sons during two days of speed technique training at the Under Armour Global Headquarters Performance Center powered by Fitness FX. Ray jumped in with his sons to do Speed Abs and the Ten-Minute Stretching Routine.

Ray Lewis doing Speed Abs super heavy crunches with 185 lbs. How to know if you have done speed abs correctly? If your abs are so exhausted with 20-heavy reps that you find it difficult to raise up because your abs are too gone to help; this means you did it correctly

Speed technique training with Ray Lewis sons, Ray, Rahsaan, and Ralin

10

Ten-Minute Stretching Routine

The most efficient way I've found over the years to implement a stretching routine that gets superior results in 3 days a week, is the Ten-Minute Stretching Routine. Here's how and why it works.

When athletes train correctly for speed and strength, they are traumatizing muscles being worked at the cellular level. This occurs way down into muscle where there are three distinct fiber types. The muscle fibers that get recruited and performs the work is actually being slightly injured -- on purpose -- because the body adapts to the training stimulus by becoming bigger and stronger as the muscle fiber heals during sleep.

Ray Lewis and sons finishing with the Ten-Minute Stretching Routine

When muscle heals stronger, it also heals back a little tighter. However, if flexibility training is added via stretching, during this process (micro-trauma to healing), muscle will become stronger and more elastic.

Speed and strength training without flexibility training during the training week is a mistake because athletes will not get everything out of the muscle they have -- unless the two are combined during this process.

It is actually positive to have tight joints as this generally means athletes are strong. But strength gains from lifting may not get applied unless athletes are getting strong AND flexible during the training-adaptation process. Athletes with flexibility that allows the body to move at its full range of motion, means athletes will get everything out of the muscle strength they have.

Many coaches have seen very strong athletes sitting on the bench because their performance doesn't match their strength. When I see this, it's almost always a case where an athlete loves lifting, but hates stretching. I'm preaching to me now. I love lifting and I hate, I mean hate, taking the time to stretch.

I explain to athletes, *plain and simple, if you don't stretch, you won't live up to your potential as an athlete.*

Stretching offers many benefits, but there is an issue about the type of stretching and the timing of stretching before training and athletic competitions. It is well established that dynamic mobility drills are preferred before training because research has shown prolonged stretching decreases strength for up to an hour after stretching by slightly impairing muscle activation, (*Reduced strength after passive stretch of the human plantar flexors*, 2000, Fowles).

Dynamic Mobility Before
Static After

Here is where the mistake is made; the common 10-second stretch hold positions do not get optimal results. Measurable gains in flexibility are dependent on the *duration of stretch-hold position*, and researchers show the best stretch-hold position (for time-spent) is *30 seconds*, (*The effect of time on static stretch on the flexibility of the hamstring muscles*, 1994, Bandy).

Best means optimal results for time-spent. You can get positive results with 2-minute stretch-holds, but 30 seconds yields equal results.

The results of another study show both *static* and *dynamic* will increase hamstring flexibility (a key component in continuing speed improvement). However, using a 30-second static stretch was more effective than dynamic for improving measurable flexibility, (*The effect of static stretch and dynamic range of motion training on the flexibility of the hamstring muscles*, 2001, Bandy).

Researchers show in another study that athletes should not perform prolonged static stretching before the big game or a key practice session because it slows muscle activation for around an hour afterwards, (*Reduced strength after passive stretch of the human plantar flexors*, 2000, Fowles).

Using dynamic flexibility like light plyos before a speed workout is a wise pre-practice and pre-competition strategy. Static stretching on the other hand builds flexibility and should be performed regularly -- just not immediately before a big game or a key practice. Ideally, static stretching should be performed immediately after practice when muscles are warm.

*Hardin County football team (above) finishing speed technique training.
Club soccer team (left) finishing speed technique training with the
Ten-Minute Stretching Routine*

How to Negate the Concrete

Society today, for the most part, lives life on concrete. Just think about how much time you spend on hard surfaces vs. soft ground. Human beings adapt to modern life on concrete by spending $80 billion a year for soft shoes with raised heels. While the soft shoes help the lower back, walking around in semi high-heel shoes causes the Achilles to get abnormally tight and the hamstrings to get very tight.

When hamstrings are too tight, they actually fight knee lift during sprinting. Over the years, parents who bring their teenage athletes to me for speed technique training are shocked at how inflexible kids are today. Most can't touch their toes in a self-measured *sit and reach* flexibility test.

Anytime I coach a small group of athletes, I force myself to lead the group in the Ten-Minute Stretching Routine. Near the end of the stretching, everyone is asked to do a self-measured (seated with both legs in front, side-by-side with straight knees) for a *sit and reach* test showing where they were when they first started the routine and where they are now.

The measurement is a self-estimated number of inches past their toes or inches needed to touch their toes with perfectly straight knees for at least three seconds. Typically, the average improvement for tight athletes is 4 inches in measurable flexibility in less than four weeks when performed 3 days a week. A rough measurement for optimal hamstring is athletes reaching past their toes approximately four to seven inches.

It's interesting, the fastest athletes on a team may have the tightest hamstrings, which means strong hamstrings, but when these athletes improve flexibility and learn speed technique, they flat-out fly.

Typically, coaches will record the initial measurement and track performance monthly. The most important benefit comes from the self-measurement and athletes see they are improving when they do this routine 3 days a week. Athletes are encouraged to self-measure each time after the *Split-Leg Stretch.*

Initial flexibility measurement at the Riekes Center, Menlo Park, CA

Optimal flexibility for the hamstring sit-and-reach is toes hitting the wrists. Football and track athlete John Campbell showing close to optimal

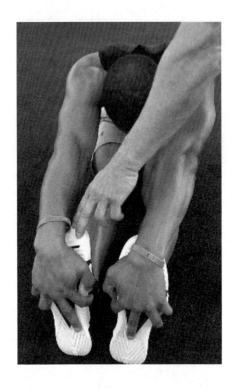

Ray Lewis III demonstrating optimal flexibility with the sit & reach hamstring flexibility self-measured test, four inches past his toes. Flexibility is a secret weapon in speed

Ten-Minute Stretching Routine

This routine is the most efficient way I can find to hit the important speed muscles, especially hamstrings that are a primary injury target of fast athletes.

All stretching positions in the Ten-Minute Stretching Routine are static, which means there should be no bouncing. Slowly move into the stretching position shown and get *fully stretched*. Athletes will know when they are fully stretched.

Almost everything done in Speed Technique 101 and 102 is fast, but with stretching, always move in-and-out stretch-hold positions in *slow motion*.

Athletes should feel slight discomfort but no sharp pain. Remain in the stretch-hold position for 30 seconds (without bouncing), and then slowly ease out of and into the next stretching position.

During the 40 years that I have been involved in coaching speed, I've noticed (here's my personal opinion, which is not backed by research) stretching is unlike other forms of exercise. Most exercises provide positive results quickly. With stretching, it's like the body fights flexibility gains for the first few weeks. After a couple of weeks, the body stops resisting and agrees to increase flexibility.

Doing this stretching program three times a week will increase your range of motion in several areas, and your gains in flexibility should become noticeable within a few weeks. Typically, tight athletes attending my speed camps will see measurable flexibility gains of four inches in four weeks with this routine.

Stretches

1. Hamstring Stretch
2. Leg Over Hip Stretch
3. Single-leg hamstring-quad sequence
   Ankle Knee-Hug Stretch
   Quad Stretch
4. Split-Leg Stretch
5. Poston Protocol
6. Achilles-Calf Stretch

1. Hamstring Stretch

Sitting on the floor with one leg extended, toes up, and the other leg bent, slowly pull forward. You will feel this in the target area -- hamstrings, calves, and lower back.

Once in the fully stretched position (there should be slight discomfort, but no real pain), remain in the stretch-hold position for 30 seconds. Yoga practitioners sometimes call this "Head to Knee" pose, which in yoga terms, means a stretching position.

Almost every muscle group receives benefit from this stretching position -- hamstrings, calves, achilles tendons, quads, obliques, shoulders, upper and lower back. This is the first stretching position and serves as a warm-up for the other more demanding stretching positions that follow.

When the hamstrings are flexible, this typically helps the other related muscle groups needing flexibility. Researchers report there is a significant increase in hamstring flexibility that can be maintained for hours when using static stretching. Muscle flexibility gains are greatest immediately after stretching.

Hamstring stretch demonstrated by Jeremy Shore, CSCS, Director of Education, Matrix Fitness USA

Researchers report:

A duration of 30 seconds is an effective time of stretching for enhancing the flexibility of the hamstring muscles. Given the information that no increase in flexibility of the hamstring muscles occurred by increasing the duration of stretching from 30 to 60 seconds, the use of the longer duration of stretching for an acute effect must be questioned, (Bandy WD (1994) *The effect of time on static stretch on the flexibility of the hamstring muscles,* Mar, Phys Ther)

2. Leg Over Hip Stretch

The move from the *hamstring stretch* to the *leg over* position is easy. Keep the left leg straight, toes up, and take the right leg and cross it over the left leg. Place the right foot near the knee. This stretching position targets the lower back, shoulders, upper back, traps, hips, groin, glutes, obliques, and even the neck muscles will feel the stretch of this position.

Leg Over Hip Stretch demonstrated by Christine Campbell

To maximize the effectiveness of this stretching position, try to twist your head as far to the right as possible. After holding this stretch for 30 seconds, slowly ease out of the position, switch legs, and repeat on the other side.

3. Right leg Stretching Sequence

The *hamstring stretching sequence* is shown below. Focus on the right hamstring first. While lying on your back, raise your right leg and with your right hand, grab your ankle (or sock, pant leg) and pull slightly to feel the hamstring stretch. Straighten your leg for a straight knee as shown below and hold for 30 seconds.

Right leg Up

Leg Over

After 30 seconds, roll the right over the left leg while looking to the right. The right knee should be straight at belt level. The goal is to hold the right knee straight so the stretch is felt. Even if the right leg has to move down toward the feet, keep the right knee straight. A bent right knee here isn't effective.

After 30 seconds, roll the right leg back up again as shown, except this time keep the *right hip (or right glute) on the surface*. During the first hamstring stretch, the hips can be open (weight on left hip). However, it's important to close the hips for this stretch by putting weight on the right hip as this targets the biceps femoris hamstring that frequently gets missed.

Knee-Hug Ankle Stretch

As part of the sequence and still working on the right leg, pull the right knee into the chest with the right hand. With the left hand, reach around the foot as shown below and actually twist the ankle toward the body. This is a prehab flexibility exercise to build flexibility protection from an ankle roll injury from stepping on an athlete's foot during practice. The goal is to prehab the ankle for a common athletic injury so it doesn't need rehab later.

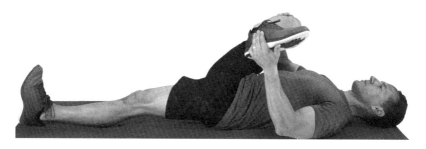

Quad stretch

Last stretch of the right leg sequence is the quad stretch. Roll to the left side and with right hand on foot, pull the quad toward the right glute for 30 seconds.

Once quad stretch is finished, the sequence begins for the left leg before moving to the Split-legs Stretch.

4. Split-Legs Stretch

There are three parts to this stretch. Start by sitting on the floor with split legs, toes up, and knees straight. Before pulling forward to the center, pull the chest toward the right knee and hold for 30 seconds as shown below by Holly Campbell. Then pull left for 30 seconds. To finish, pull forward (as shown right) for 30 seconds. Toes should be pointed up and knees straight.

Pull right position

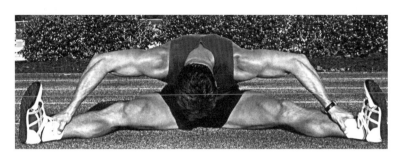

Pull forward position

5. Poston Protocol

I learned this amazingly effective protocol from Lee Poston PT, Dip, MDT, CSCS, CF-L1. While Lee gives credit to Robin McKenzie, I've referred to this as the *Poston Protocol* for years.

It looks similar to the cobra pose in Yoga. It begins with 10 reps of a press up where the hips and legs remain relaxed and on the floor. On the 10th rep, lock out elbows, take a deep breath, exhale and let the spine sag for 30 seconds. Lee Poston explains:

Studies show we sit or bend several thousand times per day. This habit starts in school as students with poor posture. When we are young and "invincible," we can get away with this bad habit - though we are seeing more cases of back pain at younger ages due to computers and video games.

The high-risk years are 30-55 due to being less active, and settling into a job that puts us in the same poor (sitting and bending) positions daily. We rarely bend backward and never to end range. All joints including the spine must have full range of motion in all directions.

We simply never check our back bend until it's too late. Sitting and bending flexion-based lifestyles cause the contents of our discs, or shock absorbers, between each vertebra to shift. This happens slowly and silently over time until an episode of back pain begins for "no apparent reason." Our flexion-based lifestyles are causing displacement to the point that people can literally be disabled from something simple like coughing, sneezing or bending down to pick up a light object.

This is simply the straw that breaks the camel's back.

If this movement produces pain out to the right or left, or it produces leg pain, this means a more serious issue needing therapy. This exercise will either fix your pain or identify the need to visit a McKenzie MDT clinician (https://www.mckenzieinstituteusa.org). You should have full and free ability to bend backward. If so, your back is healthy. If you are stiff, whether you have pain or not, pain will be coming and you should do the press ups 10 times 5-6x/day until it is full and free. (Lee Poston, outrigger70@ yahoo.com, *Interview 5/1/2019*).

If the exercise below is not at a full range of motion, athletes need to do the *Poston Protocol* several times a day for a few weeks. As explained by Lee Poston, not achieving end range low back extension (bending backward) is an indicator of forthcoming back problems.

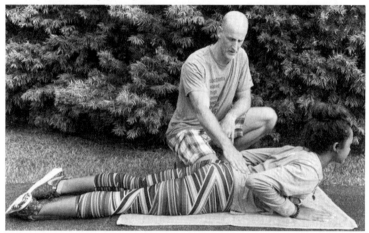

Starting position for the Poston Protocol

The starting position (above) is demonstrated by high school track & field Hawaii state champion Chenoa Frederick and Lee Poston. While keeping the hips down and in contact with the ground throughout the exercise, the athlete does 10 press ups to bend the lower back high as possible to the *up position*. After 10 press-up reps, hold the last rep up for 30 seconds.

Chenoa was suffering from severe low back pain and unable to train for her track & field events at 100% for months. Three days prior to the state championships, Chenoa met Lee Poston via Facetime 3,000 miles away.

Based on limited time, Lee used tele-health for mechanical diagnosis and he prescribed a movement treatment plan. Chenoa followed the plan and quickly experienced significant improvement in back flexibility. Lee finally met Chenoa in person the day before the state championships. He assisted her in reaching full range of motion flexion and extension with no back pain.

Did it help Chenoa during the state championships?

In the rain, Chenoa, a junior at Kamehameha Schools-Hawaii on the Big Island, won the 100-meter sprint in 12.5 seconds. She jumped 18.2 feet to win the long jump. She also won the triple jump and the high jump. I think the *Poston Protocol* helped, (https://www.hawaiiprepworld.com/featured/track-update-4-ks-hawaiis-chenoa-frederick-pours-it-on-for-4-titles/).

The press-up position during the Poston Protocol demonstrated by Chenoa Frederick

It doesn't help that many student athletes sit slightly stooped forward in the classroom and then sit and stand stooped as they look down at their smart phone hours a day. But this is reality, and as coaches, we may need to implement a counterbalance to the near constant spine flexion by using the *Poston Protocol* during practice and teaching athletes to do this one-minute exercise several times during the day.

6. Achilles - Calf Stretch

Achilles calf Stretch is the final stretch. As shown below, the body is straight with a forward lean. The back knee straight for the first 15 seconds. The final 15 seconds, keep heel on the ground and slightly bend back knee forward to target the soleus muscle that is behind the calves.

Start with back knee straight (left photo) 15 seconds.
Bend back knee (right photo) with heel on floor for 15 seconds

Ten-Minute Stretching Routine
After practice, not before

Teaching pocket-chin arms at the Riekes Center in Menlo Park, CA

11

S-Drive & S-Force

I had the privilege of writing the speed technique protocols for the Matrix S-Drive and the S-Force. These are two self-propelled athletic training units that are made affordable for coaches because they do not have motors.

In a perfect world, if I were a strength & conditioning coach (as I once was) I would have an S-Drive on one side of the lifting platform, rig/cage system with the S-Force on the other.

I designed the *S-Drive Speed Technique Protocols* to achieve mission-critical objectives necessary to improve athletic performance in sprint-running sports for a four-week period, where week 3 and 4 can be repeated indefinitely or modified by coaches to fit their training situation.

During the first four weeks, athletes will begin to internalize optimal speed techniques by performing specifically designed drills that teach optimal body positioning (proprioception), and upper and lower body sprint mechanics. Practicing correct sprint technique during training will incrementally increase practice speed and ultimately game speed for an entire team of athletes.

The protocols were designed to accomplish the following objectives:

1. The protocols direct reprogramming the brain and nervous system to recruit more fast-muscle fiber necessary for speed improvement.

2. Recruiting more fast-muscle fiber through correct body positioning and practicing optimal sprint mechanics during drills and S-Drive sprinting reps, athletes create maximum micro-trauma in the IIa and IIx fast-muscle fiber resulting in a superior adaptation to the training.

3. Recruiting the maximum amount of muscle fiber during the sprinting reps will force the heart and lungs to oxygenate more muscle fiber. This process means athletes will comprehensively condition both processes of the heart muscle - the aerobic and the anaerobic conditioning process.

Backpedal 15 steps (like a DB or outfielder) to a Hip Flip

4. Since athletic performance in most sprinting sports can be significantly improved by increasing *drive phase* performance (dead start to 20 yards), the Speed Technique Protocols focus on *drive phase* sprint reps.

5. Since the main role of the inner-ear is to keep human beings from falling, the drills and *drive phase* sprint reps in the protocols will progressively reduce the impact of *inner-ear brakes* that cause athletes to run too upright taking more steps than necessary.

6. The hormonal response of the Speed Technique Protocols accomplishes the results of the Sprint 8 Cardio Protocol, which is shown in two-hospital based studies to increase exercise-induced growth hormone significantly for enhanced muscle building and body-fat reduction.

7. Endurance capacity and enhanced energy levels for training, practice and competition comes from ATP produced by the mitochondria in the muscle cells. New research shows the best way to increase the number of muscle cell mitochondria is fast-fiber sprint cardio training.

Controlled Hip Flip to a Drive-up drill demonstrated by Zac Elliott

Matrix S-Drive Speed Technique Protocols are efficient for coaches with limited training time. The protocols multitask warm-up and the three speed technique drills to teach and rehearse *fly phase* with the *claw drill*, *drive phase* with *leg drives*, and *pocket-chin arms* for optimal arm technique for both phases.

The speed technique protocols are designed to be logistically efficient for coaches with large teams. Three to five athletes in a training group can work through the protocols in approximately 20 minutes, leaving time for platform lifting, ancillary strength training, core and flexibility training.

The *Matrix S-Drive Speed Technique Protocols* are designed to lead your athletes to achieve their maximum potential for top-end speed, maximum acceleration from a stop or change-of-direction movement, and acceleration speed bursts.

Optimal speed technique is broken down into three parts:

1. Body positioning
2. Leg action
3. Arm action

Once the three major technique drills are practiced as speed technique rehearsal during the first few minutes of the workout, speed techniques are pulled together and applied in short, sprint-running reps. Every rep introduces and reinforces technique refinement. Constructive coaching cues can be provided real-time to athletes during sprint reps because the coach is beside the athlete.

*Drive-up from bottom bar with 5 full-speed steps
on all four bars*

Advanced speed techniques are added progressively during the first four weeks like the *backpedal, hip flip, drive-up drill* that resembles many sports-specific and position-specific functional movements.

For safe entry on the S-Drive, the *Grab and Off Drill* should be performed by every athlete before sprinting on the S-Drive. This drill doesn't need to be done every workout, but every athlete needs to do two reps of this drill. Once they do, no matter how fast they sprint, they will have a safety mechanism built in.

With the harness on the S-Drive, the athlete walks against the belt for a few steps. The coach gives the commands, *walk, jog* and *grab & off*. Athletes *grab* the two side bars, and jump off straddling the treadmill with both hands on the side rails. This is a simple, but important drill every athlete needs to show a coach that he or she understands how to do the *grab & off* exit.

After the Drive-up drill, finish the rep with a 5 step, full speed, hands-free sprint

Speed Technique Protocol S-Drive - Week 1

Warm-up

Grab & off drill, two reps per athlete (Chapter 3)

Harness off, hand controls: Parachute #8, Weight PusH #8 so the belt doesn't move. The three technique drills can also be beside the S-Drive, leaning on and holding the side bar. Drills are in Chapter 3.

Technique Drills

Leg drives
Claw drill

___ 5 reps per leg, 50% speed, 75% speed, 100% speed

Pocket-chin arms

___ 5 reps arm cycle pumps at 50%, 75%, 100% speed

Warm-Up Runs

Harness ON: Parachute #1-2, Weight Push #1

___ 15-second run 50% speed

___ 10-second run 75% speed

___ 6-second run 90% speed

Fly Phase Sprinting

Harness ON: Parachute #1, Weight Push #1

SPEED TECHNIQUE FOCUS; *Pocket-chin arms*

___ 15-second 70% speed sprint

___ 10-second 90% speed sprint

___ 5-second 100% max sprint

___ 5-second 100% max sprint

Drive Phase Sprinting

Harness OFF: Parachute #1, Weight Push #1

SPEED TECHNIQUE FOCUS: *Body straight, Airplane takeoff*

__ Drive phase sprint. Hands on Low bar, 10 full-speed steps

__ DRIVE-ups rep

__ DRIVE-ups rep

__ DRIVE-ups rep

Beginning with hands on low bar, sprint 5 full-speed steps
move up one bar. Every 5 full-speed steps move hands up, bar-by-bar
moving up to the top bar, grab & off to complete Drive-up reps

Power Training

Harness OFF: Parachute #4, Weight Push #1

__ Richter Rep -10 full-speed steps (see page 120)

__ Richter Rep -10 full-speed steps

Parachute #4, Weight Push #4-5

__ Drive phase Sled Push, low bar, 15 full-speed steps

__ Sled Pull 15 steps, hip flip to Sled Push, 15 steps

Sled Pull & Push is elbows on side rails, pull backward 15 steps, hip flip
to grab low bar for drive phase Sled Push 15 full-speed steps
S-Drive Power Training can be substituted with S-Force reps

Ten-Minute Stretching Routine

Designed to target muscle groups propelling sprinting speed

Richter rep on the Matrix S-Drive

Speed Technique Protocol S-Drive - Week 2

Harness off, hand controls: Parachute #8, Weight Push #8. Three technique drills can also be beside the S-Drive, leaning on and holding the side bar.

Technique Drills
Leg drives
Claw drill
___ 5 reps per leg, 50% speed, 75% speed, 100% speed
Pocket-chin arms
___ 5 reps arm cycle pumps at 50%, 75%, 100% speed

Warm-Up Runs
Harness ON: Parachute #1-2, Weight Push #1
___ 15-second run 50% speed
___ 10-second run 75% speed
___ 6-second run 90% speed

Fly Phase Sprinting
Harness ON: Parachute #1, Weight Push #1
SPEED TECHNIQUE FOCUS; *Pocket-chin arms*
___ 12-second 70% speed sprint
___ 10-second 90% speed sprint
___ 5-second 100% max sprint
___ 5-second 100% max sprint

Drive Phase Sprinting
Harness OFF: Parachute #1, Weight Push #1
SPEED TECHNIQUE FOCUS: *Body straight, Airplane takeoff*
___ DRIVE-ups rep
___ DRIVE-ups rep
___ DRIVE-ups rep with 5 steps *pocket-chin arms* free-hand sprint
Sprint 5 full-speed steps per rung. Let go for 5 steps
of free-hand *pocket-chin arms* sprint, grab & off

Power Training

Harness OFF: Parachute #4, Weight Push #1

___ Richter Rep -10 full-speed steps (see page 120)

___ Richter Rep -10 full-speed steps

Parachute #4, Weight Push #4-8

___ Drive phase Sled Push low bar, 15 full-speed steps

___ Sled Pull 15 steps, hip flip to Sled Push, 15 steps

___ Sled Pull 15 steps, hip flip to Sled Push, 15 steps

Sled Pull & Push is elbows on side rails, pull backward 15 steps, hip flip
to grab low bar for drive phase Sled Push 15 full-speed steps

S-Drive Power Training can be substituted with S-Force reps

Strength Training

Ten-Minute Stretching Routine
Designed to target muscle groups propelling sprinting speed
(Chapter 10)

Driving the S-Drive sled with weight resistance on level 4 - 8

Speed Technique Protocol S-Drive - Week 3

Harness off, hand controls: Parachute #8, Weight Push #8. Three technique drills can also be beside the S-Drive, leaning on and holding the side bar.

Technique Drills
Leg drives
Claw drill
Pocket-chin arms

Warm-Up Runs
Harness ON: Parachute #1-2, Weight Push #1
___ 15-second run 50% speed
___ 10-second run 75% speed
___ 6-second run 90% speed

Fly Phase Sprinting
Harness ON: Parachute #1, Weight Push #1
SPEED TECHNIQUE FOCUS; *Pocket-chin arms*
___ 12-second 70% speed sprint
___ 10-second 90% speed sprint
___ 5-second 100% max sprint
___ 5-second 100% max sprint

Drive Phase Sprinting
Harness OFF: Parachute #1, Weight Push #1
SPEED TECHNIQUE FOCUS: *Body straight, Airplane takeoff*
___ DRIVE-ups rep
___ DRIVE-ups rep with 5 steps, free-hand sprint
___ DRIVE-ups rep with 5 steps, free-hand sprint
Sprint 5 full-speed steps bottom bar up. Let go for 5 steps
of free-hand *pocket-chin arms* sprint, grab & off

Functional Sports Specific Training

__ Back pedal 15 steps, hip flip to bottom bar Drive-up drill
with a 5 step, free-hand, *pocket-chin arms* sprint
__ Back pedal 15 steps, hip flip to bottom bar Drive-up drill
with a 5 step, free-hand, *pocket-chin arms* sprint
Note: Sports-specific, position-specific drills added here

Power Training

Harness OFF: Parachute #4, Weight Push #1
__ Richter Rep - 10 full-speed steps (see page 120)
__ Richter Rep -10 full-speed steps
Parachute #4, Weight Push #4-8
__ Drive phase Sled Push, low bar, 15 full-speed steps
__ Sled Pull 15 steps, hip flip to Sled Push, 15 steps
__ Sled Pull 15 steps, hip flip to Sled Push, 15 steps
Sled Pull & Push is elbows on side rails, pull backward 15 steps, hip flip
to grab low bar for drive phase Sled Push 15 full-speed steps
S-Drive Power Training can be substituted with S-Force reps

Strength Training

Ten-Minute Stretching Routine

Designed to target muscle groups propelling sprinting speed

NOTE: After four weeks of S-Drive Speed Technique training,
Week 3 and 4 are repeated, or coaches can format to suit their situation

Speed Technique Protocol S-Drive - Week 4

Harness off, hand controls: Parachute #8, Weight Push #8. Three technique drills can also be beside the S-Drive, leaning on and holding the side bar.

Technique Drills
Leg drives
Claw drill
Pocket-chin arms

Warm-Up Runs
Harness ON: Parachute #1-2, Weight Push #1
___ 15-second run 50% speed
___ 10-second run 75% speed
___ 6-second run 90% speed

Fly Phase Sprinting
Harness ON: Parachute #1, Weight Push #1
SPEED TECHNIQUE FOCUS; *Pocket-chin arms*
___ 12-second 70% speed sprint
___ 10-second 90% speed sprint
___ 5-second 100% max sprint
___ 5-second 100% max sprint

Drive Phase Sprinting
Harness OFF: Parachute #1, Weight Push #1
SPEED TECHNIQUE FOCUS: *Body straight, Airplane takeoff*
___ DRIVE-ups rep
___ DRIVE-ups rep with 5 steps, free-hand sprint
___ DRIVE-ups rep with 5 steps, free-hand sprint
Sprint 5 full-speed steps bottom bar up. Let go for 5 steps
of free-hand *pocket-chin arms* sprint, grab & off

NOTE: After four weeks of S-Drive Speed Technique training,
Week 3 and 4 are repeated, or coaches can format to suit their situation

Functional Sports Specific Training

__ Back pedal 15 steps, hip flip to bottom bar Drive-up drill
with a 5 step, free-hand, *pocket-chin arms* sprint

__ Back pedal 15 steps, hip flip to bottom bar Drive-up drill
with a 5 step, free-hand, *pocket-chin arms* sprint

Note: Sports-specific, position-specific drills added here

Power Training

Harness OFF: Parachute #4, Weight Push #1

__ Richter Rep - 10 full-speed steps (see page 120)

__ Richter Rep -10 full-speed steps

Parachute #4, Weight Push #4-8

__ Drive phase Sled Push, low bar, 15 full-speed steps

__ Sled Pull 15 steps, hip flip to Sled Push, 15 steps

__ Sled Pull 15 steps, hip flip to Sled Push, 15 steps

Sled Pull & Push is elbows on side rails, pull backward 15 steps, hip flip
to grab low bar for drive phase Sled Push 15 full-speed steps

S-Drive Power Training can be substituted with S-Force reps

Strength Training

Ten-Minute Stretching Routine

Designed to target muscle groups propelling sprinting speed

S-Drive can be used for track & field long jump

Matrix S-Force

S-Force HIIT Protocols execute mission-critical objectives necessary to improve athletic acceleration in sprint-running sports.

Designed specifically with the strength & conditioning coach and performance trainer in mind, the high-intensity interval training protocols combine the benefits of the *Sprint 8 Cardio Protocol* program with a variety of interval lengths and HIIT ladders to push athletes to superior performance.

Count on these intense protocols to trigger the release of natural human growth hormone, helping athletes burn fat and build muscle in a way that gives them a real performance edge. Combine these protocols with a range of strength training exercises to maximize the benefits of this hormone release will help athletes reach their ultimate physical potential.

Coach Nick Nguyen shows how Matrix S-Force places athletes in the speed burst acceleration position with a straight body, chin down, high knees, forward lean. This is the optimal position for a superior neurological adaptation while working all three muscle-fiber types used in sprint-running sports

S-Force Goals

Improvement in athletic performance occurs in several ways:

1. The S-Force protocols directly reprogram the brain and nervous system to recruit fast-twitch muscle fiber necessary for speed improvement.

2. By recruiting more fast-twitch muscle fiber through correct body positioning and perfected mechanics during sprinting reps, athletes create maximum micro-trauma in the fast-twitch fiber, resulting in a superior adaptation to the training.

3. Recruiting the maximum amount of muscle fiber during the sprinting reps will force the heart and lungs to oxygenate more muscle fiber. This means athletes will comprehensively condition the aerobic and anaerobic processes of the heart muscle.

4. Since athletic performance in most sprinting sports can be significantly improved by increasing drive-phase performance, the S-Force protocols continually place athletes in ideal acceleration position.

5. Since one of the main roles of the inner-ear is to keep human beings from falling, doing S-Force sprint reps in the acceleration position progressively reduces the impact of *inner-ear brakes* that cause athletes to run too upright and take more steps than necessary.

6. The hormonal response to the S-Force protocols accomplishes the goals to receive the benefits of the Sprint 8 Cardio Protocol, which two hospital-based studies have shown to increase exercise-induced human growth hormone, significantly enhancing the ability to build muscle and burn fat.

7. Adenosine triphosphate (ATP) produced by mitochondria growth in the muscle cells from this type of sprint training provides enhanced endurance and energy levels for training, practice and competition. Research shows the best way to increase the number of ATP-producing mitochondria is fast-muscle fiber recruiting sprint cardio training (Chapter 1).

S-Force Sprint 8

S-Force Sprint 8: Warm-up can be ground based or on the S-Force doing three varied stride lengths from quarter strides, half and full strides.

Rep	SPRINT	INTENSITY	RECOVERY
1	15 seconds	100% speed	90 seconds
2	15 seconds	100% speed	90 seconds
3	15 seconds	100% speed	90 seconds
4	15 seconds	100% speed	90 seconds
5	15 seconds	100% speed	90 seconds
6	15 seconds	100% speed	90 seconds
7	15 seconds	100% speed	90 seconds
8	15 seconds	100% speed	90 seconds

HIIT 10 / 20 / 30 seconds 1:4 Protocol

With a work to recovery ratio of 1:4, these three protocols are demanding. The HIIT 10 (for 10-second sprints; 40 second recovery) is suitable for most athletes. The HIIT 30 with 30-second sprints is suitable for long-distance endurance athletes.

Warm-up can be ground based or on the S-Force doing three varied stride lengths from quarter strides, half and full strides.

The recovery period is a 1 to 4 ratio for a total of 8 reps. Should the cardio sprint be 10 seconds the active recovery is 40 seconds. The 20-second sprint, the recovery would be 80 seconds, and a 30-second sprint would have a 2-minute recovery.

HIIT 10 / 1:4   8 reps of 10-second sprints, 40-seconds recovery

HIIT 20 / 1:4   8 reps of 20-second sprints, 80-seconds recovery

HIIT 30 / 1:4   8 reps of 30-second sprints, 2-minutes recovery

The Beast S-Force HIIT Ladder

Full-speed sprint to active recovery ratio 1:3. Warm-up can be ground based or on the S-Force

REP	SPRINT	INTENSITY	RECOVERY
1	10 seconds	100% speed	30 seconds
2	20 s	100%	60 s
3	30 s	100%	90 s
4	20 s	100%	60 s
5	10 s	100%	30 s
6	20 s	100%	60 s
7	30 s	100%	90 s
8	20 s	100%	cool down

S-Force Endurance Ladder

Warm-up can be ground based or on the S-Force doing three varied stride lengths from quarter strides, half and full strides.

REP	SPRINT	INTENSITY	RECOVERY
1	8 seconds	100% speed	20 seconds
2	15	100%	30 s
3	30	100%	90 s
4	8	100%	20 s
5	15	100%	30 s
6	30	100%	90 s
7	8	100%	20 s
8	15	100%	30 s
9	30	100%	90 s
10	8	100%	20 s
11	15	100%	30 s
12	30	100%	90 s

Athletes demonstrating speed technique training on the Matrix S-Drive during IHRSA

Marian University strength & conditioning coaches going through Speed Technique Coach Specialization training

12

Sore Muscles & Injury Prevention

When athletes feel severe muscle soreness from overtraining and their muscles are sore-to-touch, this means the muscles are swollen and actually leaking proteins from muscles into the bloodstream. Athletes attempting to perform quick, powerful movements with weakened muscle fiber is the cause of many muscular injuries.

If an athlete tries to sprint fast or makes a hard change-of-direction cut on sore-to-touch muscles, this increases the risk of injury. The risk goes up because the muscles can be as much as 50% weaker than normal. Athletes are in a higher risk of injury category when they are in a weakened state from lack of sleep, dehydration, and have sore-to-touch muscles.

Researcher Dr. Priscilla Clarkson at the University of Massachusetts used bicep curls to induce severe muscle soreness. The testing showed there was a 50% loss of strength, and strength did not return to normal for several days.

Lactic acid does not cause soreness

Lactic acidosis does not cause muscle soreness as once thought. Dr. Deborah Riebe, professor at the University of Rhode Island reports:

> *Experts agree soreness felt one to two days after a workout is partially caused by structural damage to muscle fibers. Dr. W. Stauber and colleagues used a high-powered microscope to analyze muscle fibers after an intense workout. It was clear that cell membranes ruptured and other structural components were disrupted. However, Clarkson reports the damage to muscle fibers is relatively small, with less than 5% of the tissue affected. Damage is not limited to one area, but occurs throughout the muscle fiber.*

Microscopic muscle damage causes an inflammatory response and this process contributes to muscle soreness in two ways. The accumulation of fluid (swelling) causes pressure and white blood cells, which serves as a defense system in the body, enter muscle fibers to secrete chemicals that activate pain receptors, (Byrnes and Clarkson, 1986; Smith, 1991).

Although the causes of soreness are not fully understood, scientists have eliminated some factors once thought to cause muscle soreness. It was long believed lactic acid (technically, hyperlactatemia with low blood pH or acidosis) caused soreness. Lactic acid does not cause soreness as it dissipates from muscle shortly after exercise and is not present when muscle soreness develops.

The upside and downside of training

Whether it's throwing a baseball, batting a softball, kicking a soccer ball, making a dig shot two inches above the volleyball court, running down a tennis ball in deep court, shooting a 3, or practicing a drive block, improvement in athletic performance comes from very specific training that creates micro-fiber tears in the slow, fast, and super-fast fiber and this causes the muscles, when sleeping, to grow stronger. The micro-trauma in the muscles being trained is positive, however, soreness can be a by-product of intense training.

The goal of speed training after athletes learn optimal speed technique for their positions is to apply stress to muscles and intentionally create micro-tears so the muscles heal back bigger and stronger during sleep.

Sometimes speed training will create too many tears from the current level of strength and muscles experience minor soreness. A significant amount of micro-trauma can result in severe soreness (sore-to-touch after warm-up) and these muscles are in a weakened injury-prone state as much as 50% weaker than normal.

Whether it's Dr. Hans Selye's *General Adaptation Syndrome* in the 1950s, or Dr. Julius Wolff's, father of *Wolff's Law* way back in 1882, it has been consistently proven that the human body adapts to the way it's trained.

Dr. Wolff demonstrated that bone in a healthy person will adapt to the loads under which it is placed. If loading on a bone increases, the bone will remodel itself over time to become stronger to support that load. The opposite is also true. If the normal loading on a bone decreases, the bone will become less dense and weaker due to lack of load.

This causes major issues for athletes healing injury off-their-feet in only a few weeks. We can learn from research on astronauts who lose 1% to 2% of their bone density every month in space. Some studies show the loss can be as much as 5% a month. The take home for coaches is when athletes are out with an injury that kept them from putting weight on their legs like calf, achilles, hamstring, and quad injuries, just know these athletes have bones that are 1% to 5% weaker. If muscles are sore-to-touch after warm-up, they are as much as 50% weaker than normal.

Above is the science, now the art of coaching enters the picture in light of the research. While sore muscles heal faster if you take the next day off, it is thought that exercising light during recovery will make muscles more fibrous so they can withstand more pressure during the next intense workout. For this reason, a training schedule of *heavy / light / heavy / light / off*, or *two days on, one day off* may be optimal. Clearly, both methods provide recovery for positive muscle adaptation to occur.

The art of coaching means that coaches can use soreness as a barometer to assess if the muscle *recovery/sleep/healing* process has taken place. Personally, I ask athletes if they have *sore-to-touch hamstrings* after the general warm-up. It they are sore-to-touch after warm-up, they shouldn't go full speed that day or risk a serious hamstring pull.

How do your hamstrings feel, are they tender to touch? These types of questions are good to ask after warm-up to determine strength/weakness status. There may be some minor soreness before the warm-up. Frequently, minor soreness will be gone after the warm-up. However, if hamstrings are tender to touch after warm-up or described as *really tight,* this means the athlete could be one quick movement away from a season-ending hamstring injury.

The act of stretching doesn't prevent injury. Improved flexibility from stretching over time helps lower risk of injury

Stretching during the training week helps keep muscles elastic and this helps to reduce the risk of muscular injury.

A weak muscle at the time a hard and fast movement is made is what causes injury because the muscle isn't strong enough to handle the demand placed on it at that moment. It's not caused by the lack of stretching during the warm-up. Lack of recovery and sleep while continuing to stress sore muscles in a weakened state is what sets athletes up for injury.

When a set of muscles is weak, like hamstrings and quads, that work together to support ligaments in the knee, hard cuts on weakened leg muscles create a dangerous situation for ACLs. Successful ACL prevention strategies include strengthening the muscles surrounding and supporting the knees. Continuing to sprint-run athletes on weakened, sore muscles means they don't have the strength to support knee ligaments as they do normally.

Athletes don't realize the danger of injury is present when the motivation of competition kicks in. If a soccer athlete for example, makes a hard-lateral cut in a weakened state, the muscle fails to perform its job in supporting knee movement, and the ACL can't handle the pressure, this can cause the ACL to tear.

ACL tears in female soccer athletes are more common than they should be. A simple ACL test can be conducted with female athletes to begin the proprioception training of how to keep knee ligaments from being placed into an injury prone valgus position.

Athletes stand in front of a mirror and step off a bench to personally observe how their knees react when catching their body weight. If the knees stay straight and bend toward the toes without going inward (valgus), this is positive and the correct way to land (below, center photo).

If the knees naturally go into the valgus position briefly (bottom right) to catch the athlete's jump, this is a big red-light indicator of a potential ACL injury requiring surgical repair unless the athlete understands the problem and learns how she must fix the problem. Athletes must retrain their brain not to go valgus. This is another way the *exercise paradox* impacts athletes. The brain uses the skeleton and ligaments rather than tired muscles to support athletic movements.

Jump from a bench   *Correct knees when landing*   *Incorrect valgus knees when landing*

Misunderstood role of warm-up in preventing injury

A general warm-up followed by a sports-specific and position-specific warm-up that progressively brings muscles up to work mode makes the muscles much stronger than when muscles are at rest.

This type of progressive warm-up process helps to reduce the risk of injury. The warm-up itself doesn't prevent injury. The warm-up prepares muscles by getting them into work mode.

Knowing what causes weakened-state muscles will help reduce the risk of injury. *Dehydration* makes muscles weak. Whether it's caused by lack of fluid & electrolytes, heat, direct sunlight (that can dehydrate the skin for days), decongestants, popular stimulant drinks, and ADHD medications, this weakens muscle. Adding dehydration to sore muscles is a disaster waiting to happen, especially with hard working athletes who practice fast.

Some coaches are beginning to treat *salty sweaters* with salt tablets after practice. Many athletes sweat out more salt in their sweat than others. For coaches who practice athletes in hot environments like the south during August, managing heavy sweating is part of the job description. This question can be asked, *do your eyes burn when you sweat?* Some athletes will answer no. These athletes don't get dehydrated as often, and they don't generally cramp.

Athletes who answer, *yes, my eyes burn when I sweat*, will be the athletes who tend to get dehydrated quicker because they sweat more salt out than others. Coaches can even see the white salt on dark shirts. *Salty Sweaters* will be your crampers. These will be the athletes that get weakened, injury-prone muscles quicker than others. These are the athletes that can rip a hamstring or an achilles off the bone when they try hard to make a fast move in a weakened state. These are the athletes who can tear an ACL with a simple lateral movement on the third day of practice in the heat.

Note, this doesn't mean that *salty sweater* athletes are necessarily working harder than others, or they are out-of-condition. It means that they simply sweat more salt out of their bodies than others.

Salty sweaters need sports drinks often, not just water, but sport drinks with salts, such as sodium, chloride, and potassium added to the fluid.

The Salt Fix: Why the Experts Got It All Wrong-and How Eating More Might Save Your Life by Dr. James DiNicolantonio and his book with Dr. Jason Fung, *The Longevity Solution: Rediscovering Centuries-Old Secrets to a Healthy, Long Life (pp. 148-163)* are highly recommended so you will have correct information about how salt and magnesium can help heavy-sweating athletes.

Rhabdo

Rhabdo (rhabdomyolysis) happens too often in college sports at the hand of a very small number of coaches who perhaps should not be coaching young athletes. PhD directors of exercise physiology related programs and accrediting organizations should teach young coaches not to become the coach with the *we run them until someone collapses* attitude, which is nothing less than premeditated intent to harm athletes.

Look at how many large athletes in football have died and how many have been sent to the hospital with rhabdo in recent years. It's shameful.

As a former Associate A.D., I would like to appeal to my A.D. colleagues, to weed the *run them until someone collapses* coach out before you and your school is sued. This attitude is totally contradictory to science about how endurance is improved and strength is gained. Endurance comes from mitochondria growth and strength comes from strategically working all three muscle-fiber types followed by adequate rest and recovery. When a coach aspires to *run athletes until someone collapse,* this is premeditated intent to harm athletes for which head coaches and A.D.s are responsible.

I am not saying go easy. To the contrary, speed training and the Sprint 8 Cardio Protocol for coaches and adults of all ages are extremely demanding. However, these workouts are not hard to stroke my ego. They are designed to create the maximum amount of micro-trauma in the muscles for a superior adaptation during sleep while conditioning the aerobic and anaerobic processes of the heart muscle for a high-quality, energy-filled life.

I am saying running large football athletes until someone drops means the coach is leading athletes to train with very sloppy speed technique in the slow-fiber endurance energy system. And these large, quick, short-sprint athletes are being trained to run more like marathon runners than football athletes. Running athletes until someone drops makes absolutely no sense.

Coach Mitch Kothe working on fly phase pocket-chin arms technique (above) and using sprint training to add mitochondria, the source of endurance, in preparation for a Spartan competition

Dr. Shail Singh, Medical Director for Sprint 8 Cardio Protocol research projects sprinting on the Matrix treadmill where Sprint 8 is the featured HIIT program

13

Sprint Cardio for Busy Coaches

Since speed training recruits all three muscle-fiber types, it burns body fat quickly and effectively. It helps athletes *of all ages* to achieve numerous desirable physical changes. It will also improve several key health measures, (Burt, D. (2012) *Targeting exercise-induced growth hormone release: A novel approach to fighting obesity by substantially increasing endogenous GH serum levels naturally*).

I created the *Sprint 8 Cardio Protocol* about 30 years ago to mimic the benefits athletes achieve when doing speed training regularly, except for one important point. Sprint 8 can be done by time-crunched coaches in a safer-on-the-hamstrings mode. Sprint 8 can be done on typical cardio machines available in most fitness centers today.

While Sprint 8 looks like HIIT training, Sprint 8 is actually a higher level of intensity called SIT (Sprint Interval Training). Sprint 8 is significantly more demanding than the current interpretation of HIIT, which seems to have evolved into a hard, slow-fiber recruiting, oscillating, on-and-off, work-recovery format.

Since Sprint 8 can be done riding a machine, the time of the cardio sprint is longer than sprint running. It's a 30-second cardio sprint when on a cardio machine, and the active recovery is always 90 seconds in between the sprints.

Here's how to know if it's truly Sprint 8 intensity -- if you can go longer than 30 seconds, don't count it. If you ever think you need to do more than 8 reps, you didn't do it right. The fully mature Sprint 8 is 8 reps of all-out, no pacing, fast-as-you-can-go (with resistance where the work is hard and fast) cardio sprint where you become totally exhausted in 30 seconds or less.

Researchers report on the efficiency and rapid improvement produced by sprint-intensity cardio:

> *A novel type of high-intensity interval training known as sprint interval training has demonstrated increases in aerobic and anaerobic performance with very low time commitment ... Our results suggest that intense interval training is indeed a time-efficient strategy to induce rapid metabolic and performance adaptations,* (Bayati M. (2011) *A practical model of low-volume high-intensity interval training induces performance and metabolic adaptations that resemble 'all-out' sprint interval training. J Sports Sci Med. 2011 Sep 1;10(3):571-6.).*

Why Sprint 8 Works

Unlike slow and moderate-intensity training, and even typical forms of interval training that have higher intensity intervals lasting longer than 30 seconds, a real Sprint 8 stimulates a huge natural release of growth hormone.

Please note that this isn't just a small release of this powerful hormone (so powerful that it determines how tall we become). It's a huge release.

While higher levels of exercise intensity offer many benefits, including a higher caloric burn rate, it is this natural stimulation of human growth hormone that has superior benefits. Elevated levels of human growth hormone are associated with increased lean muscle mass, decreased body fat and higher energy, (Godfrey, Madgwick, Whyte. (2003) *The exercise-induced growth hormone response in athletes.* Sports Medicine. 33(8):599-613).

This level of increase in exercise-induced growth hormone triggers dramatic physical transformations in normal people, who wish to lose some body fat, and in the very fit population, who are lean and mean as well, (Burt, D. (2012) *Targeting exercise-induced growth hormone release: A novel approach to fighting obesity by substantially increasing endogenous GH serum levels naturally).*

Growth hormone is produced by the pituitary gland, which is called the master gland because of its importance. This is the same hormone that makes us grow taller. Just think about this for a moment. Think about how powerful this substance is in the body. It determines how tall we become. Once we reach our full height, the hormone is the same substance, but it changes roles. Distinguished researcher, Dr. Thomas Welbourne, LSU Medical Center, says it should be called your *Fitness Hormone.*

The exciting news is that you don't have to inject this hormone to receive its benefits. The Sprint 8 Protocol can be the personal tool for time-crunched coaches to get this huge NATURAL injection of this very powerful hormone when doing Sprint 8 three days a week.

Growth hormone does many important health related things in the body. It helps to regulate body composition, muscle and bone growth, sugar and fat metabolism, and it's shown to possibly have an important role in heart function. The body releases growth hormone when you are in deep sleep and the body releases a significant amount of this powerful hormone during Sprint 8. Researchers report:

Growth hormone (GH) regulates whole body metabolism, and physical exercise is the most potent stimulus to induce its secretion in humans, *(Ignacio D. (2015, Apr 13) Thyroid hormone and estrogen regulate exercise-induced growth hormone release).*

Sprint Intensity Cardio

Sprint intensity is the secret to the clinical successes of the Sprint 8 Protocol. Sprint-intensity exercise is not easy, but it is the factor that yields the best results in the shortest time. The human body is amazing. It has the ability to respond to the challenges it faces. If someone lies around all day on the sofa watching television, the body adapts to the way it's trained (or not trained in this case) and the body turns into a puffy couch potato.

Likewise, if you train like a sprinter with the Sprint 8 Protocol on a safe gym cardio machine, your body adapts to training by becoming more like a sprinter's body. Coaches doing sprint-intensity cardio can bring an intense change in the body's composition.

When using Sprint 8 as a tool, you are forcing the body to recruit and build all three *muscle-fiber types* just like speed technique training does for athletes. The by-product is a significant release of exercise-induced growth hormone.

Everyone knows they need to exercise regularly. Time barriers for coaches with life outside of coaching are what trips up most coaches.

Sprint 8 is a weapon for time-crunched coaches and parents. It allows you to pack a huge amount of training productivity into a very short time frame.

The Sprint 8 Protocol provides the ability for coaches and parents to get fit and stay fit even with hectic schedules. Researchers report:

> *Sprint Interval Training (SIT) improves aerobic capacity in healthy, young people. Relative to continuous endurance training of moderate intensity, SIT presents an equally **effective alternative with a reduced volume of activity,*** (Gist N. (2014 Feb). *Sprint interval training effects on aerobic capacity: a systematic review and meta-analysis. Sports Med. 44(2):269-79).*

Growth Hormone & Gains

Growth hormone has a tremendously beneficial effect on the human physique. Growth hormone effectively fights the symptoms of aging, obesity, increased body fat, and less than desirable energy levels, but it also increases lean muscle. Elevated levels of growth hormone are associated with increased lean mass, muscle tone, decreased body fat, fewer wrinkles and higher energy.

Studies show that growth hormone can boost lean mass by 8.8% while lowering body fat by 14%. Growth hormone is not only the hormone that determines how tall we grow, it is able to create a dramatic change in the body that causes muscle to grow and fat to melt at the same time, (*New England Journal of Medicine*, 1990).

Growth hormone is such a powerful substance. It can make many positive changes in the body. When you are able to get growth hormone circulating with an exercise-induced release in your system, great things begin to happen to your physique, (Pritzlaff, (1990 Aug). *Impact of acute exercise intensity on pulsatile growth hormone release in men. Journal of Applied Physiology.* Aug;87(2):498-504).

When comparing the impact of exercise-induced growth hormone from the Sprint 8 Protocol in an eight-week study, a group of test subjects weighing on average 194 pounds experienced a drop in body fat of 22.39 pounds while gaining 13.39 pounds of lean mass. That's a significant gain in lean mass while cutting body fat at the same time.

Their average weight went from 194 to 185 pounds in eight weeks of Sprint 8, three-times-a-week and without changing diet (so it would not be a variable in the study). The average body-fat loss in this group classified as the *General Population Group* (of those wanting to improve health, reduce body fat, and lose more than 10 pounds) clearly shows they achieved their goals. The average drop in body fat was 27.8%. One of the physicians on the panel said *the only way you get more body fat off than this, is to cut it off.*

Sprint 8 takes you out of a calorie-counting world when it comes to results and places you in a world of injecting hormones at an anti-aging center, except, Sprint 8 is all natural.

Step out of a Calorie-Counting World

A reduction in body fat of 27% in two studies, in eight weeks, without dieting, is near unbelievable. I know it is, but I continually hear and see these results repeated. The results come from 20 minutes, three-times-a-week, sprint-intensity cardio performed the right way.

When looking at the results of the Sprint 8 Protocol, it's more like comparing results from injecting powerful hormones and steroids than comparing to traditional long / slow cardio exercise.

In fact, when the Sprint 8 studies were designed, they were based on the premise that Sprint 8 will mimic the results of injecting growth hormone, which gets an average reduction in body fat of 14.4%. When the results of both hospital-based studies came back with an average drop in body fat of *27%;* I was shocked. This means that the exercise method, the totally natural method (Sprint 8, three-times-a-week for eight weeks), is almost twice as effective in reducing body fat as injecting growth hormone daily.

Melissa Waters, R.D. with a M.S. in Nutrition from the University of North Dakota analyzed the research data. She reported when comparing the body-fat-reducing results of Sprint 8 with burning calories from exercise, ***you can do Sprint 8, 20 minutes OR get the same results by doing cardio three hours-a-day for at 75% intensity***.

Sprint 8 is a no-brainer for healthy people in the general population. Not only does Sprint 8 get superior results for the *General Population Group,* it gets great results for those who are very fit. Eight weeks of Sprint 8 in a group of fit people (*Fit Group*) who wanted to improve health, trim body fat without dieting, and weight loss wasn't a priority, also achieved their goals.

The *Fit Group* gained 1.28 pounds of lean mass, and they reduced their body fat by 13.9% without changing their diets

If I asked you take your choice of 20 minutes -- of which 4 minutes is sprint-intensity cardio and 16 minutes is casual-paced recovery, OR 75% intensity cardio for 3 hours on those same three days, my hunch is most coaches would choose 20 minutes, three-days-a-week.

Just like speed technique training for athletes, Sprint 8 forces adults of all ages to recruit all three *muscle-fiber types* to propel the exercise, whereas most forms of cardio exercise only recruit the slow type I muscle fiber. Interval training typically only recruits the fast-IIa muscle fiber and, while hard, it generally doesn't recruit the super-fast IIx muscle fiber that lays dormant.

In revolutionary research published by the *National Institutes of Health,* Dr. Richard Godfrey, a distinguished researcher at Brunel University in London introduces an entirely new approach that departs from the "calories burned" typical way of thinking about exercise productivity.

Dr. Godfrey is a senior lecturer in Sports Coaching and Human Performance. His research is in the area of human growth hormone and specifically the exercise-induced growth hormone response to exercise. Dr. Godfrey concludes:

> The impact of some of the negative effects of aging could be reduced **if exercise focused on promoting exercise produced growth hormone,** (Godfrey. R. *The exercise-induced growth hormone response in athletes.* Sports Med. 2003;33(8):599-613).

Dr. Godfrey is an expert in exercise-induced growth hormone and he does the Sprint 8. He commented, *I have also been able to use the **energy boost** this type of training has given me to get back into some 'proper' sports training.*

Training at an all-out, sprint-intensity level requires maximum physical and mental involvement. And it requires pushing the body hard, as hard as you can.

However, the upside is huge. You get your workouts over with quickly and you also get to the reward faster (less body fat, more muscle, thicker skin, thicker bones, and a lot more energy for life), and it doesn't take an hour in the gym every day. In our busy society, this is a huge plus factor.

Sprint Intensity Performed Safely

An important goal of this book is to give you tools to get your athletes faster and to give time-crunched coaches a tool to improve health and fitness in 20 minutes three day a week.

It's always a good idea to have your physician clear you for anaerobic exercise before starting sprint cardio, or any new exercise program -- especially if you have been sedentary. The goal is to strengthen your heart muscle, not harm it. If someone has clogged arteries, does high-intensity exercise, and the blood can't flow, it can significantly damage the heart muscle.

Researchers report about the effectiveness of a 30-second cardio sprint:

> The study results agree with the **effectiveness of a 30 second all-out training program** with a reduced time commitment for anthropometric, aerobic and anaerobic adaptation **and eliminate doubts about its safety as a model,** (Nalcakan GR. The Effects of Sprint Interval vs. Continuous Endurance Training on Physiological and Metabolic Adaptations in Young Healthy Adults. J Hum Kinet. 2014 Dec 30;44:97-109).

The researchers also learned this type of training suppresses the hormone that makes us hungry, *ghrelin*. In another study, researchers show that *stem cells* are increased in muscles with elevated growth hormone:

> Growth hormone may play an additional role in skeletal muscle by regulation of stem cells, as **increased stem cell numbers are found in human muscle with increased growth hormone levels**, (Heinemeier, KM. (2012, Mar 1). GH/IGF-I axis and matrix adaptation of the musculotendinous tissue to exercise in humans. Sc and J Med Sci Sports).

Amazing Human Performance Potential

Comparing the peak performance of aging track & field sprinters shows what the potential is for all human beings as they age (if they use sprint-intensity cardio in their fitness training). The results are quite amazing.

From the viewpoint of speed and peak performance, the graphic shows for every five years of life, peak performance goes down. But this is extremely positive because it only goes down *a little*.

To see human potential, look at the following graphic and compare age group World Records (in tenths) with the current 100-meter track World Record.

Age Group 100m World Records Compared to Current World Record

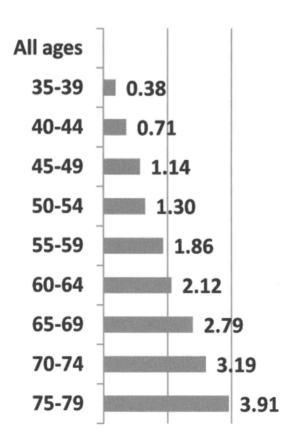

All ages	
35-39	0.38
40-44	0.71
45-49	1.14
50-54	1.30
55-59	1.86
60-64	2.12
65-69	2.79
70-74	3.19
75-79	3.91

Just look at the graphic and compare the 60 to 65-year-old masters sprinter in terms of fitness and performance with the best of the best in different age groups. The chart shows the 60-year-old masters World Record holder is only 1.78 tenths-of-a-second behind the finish line of his 35-year-old counterpart.

Now think about this. At age 60, this man is only 2.12 tenths-of-a-second slower than the current world record holder Usain Bolt, who ran 100 meters in 9.58 seconds in his early 20s. Think about the profound significance of his potential and performance.

Visualize this; Usain Bolt finishes the race, then count *one-thousand one, one-thousand two,* and boom, the 60-year-old sprints across the finish line.

Even better, Usain Bolt crosses the finish line, then count *one-thousand one, one-thousand two* and before you can finish *one-thousand three,* a 65-year-old sprints past the finish line.

Compare this 60-year-old and 65-year-old to most men their ages. Many in their 60's have trouble casual-pace walking and are a primary target of companies selling them a death trap -- a motorized wheelchair type machine that will further erode their muscle and bone density. Don't walk away from these machines. Don't run away from these machines. Sprint away! Instead, buy a cardio machine with Sprint 8 that's made for Sprint 8 intensity.

These age group world records clearly show us the potential we have for fitness and performance during aging. None of these masters sprinters will make the Olympic Team, but just think of the human potential, or better, think of the potential *YOU* have if you add sprint-intensity cardio to your training plan and keep it for a lifetime.

At age 75, when many are headed to the nursing home, this graph clearly makes the case for the human potential to be at such a level of health and fitness that a 75-year-old is only 3.91 tenths-of-a-second behind the 100-meter world record. Think about that.

At age 75, I'll take that deal all day long!

Case Study, Dr. Derick Phan

Dr. Derick Phan uses Sprint 8 training to improve his performance. Dr. Phan is a busy orthodontist and high school volleyball coach in San Jose, California. He did the two-session speed technique training, and he joined the Sprint 8 class.

Derick began running the 60-meter sprint in masters track & field events in a time of 8.31 seconds at age 40 in Rhode Island. He dropped his 60m sprint time to 7.99 in Budapest, Hungary (below right).

While most athletes see their performance times slightly slow down every year after age 40, Dr. Phan has gotten faster. Continuing to attend the Sprint 8 class three days a week to strengthen all three muscle-fiber types, he ran a 7.96 at age 42. At age 44, he ran a 7.68, which proves great things happen when athletes continue strengthening fast-muscle fiber with sprint-intensity cardio for life.

To see true human potential, visualize Christian Coleman crossing the finish line to set a new 60m World Record in 6.37. Before you say *one-thousand*, this 44-year old orthodontist is crossing the line. Think about the great things he is doing for his health and his increased energy levels for life.

This is the definition of *healthy aging.* Dr. Phan's performance continues to improve and his jumps are getting longer every year. Obviously, sprinters will slow-down slightly as they age. But Derick Phan is showing us the power of working *fast-muscle fiber* and tapping into all the body has to offer with exercise-induced growth hormone produced by sprint-intensity cardio.

Dr. Phan said, *Sprint 8 has helped me transform from a 42-year-old orthodontist to a Masters All American sprinter in just a few short months.*

While weight loss wasn't a primary goal for Dr. Phan (like it is for most people), he is one of the lean and mean in the Sprint 8 Challenge *Fit Group.* He gained 2.4 pounds of muscle and dropped 3.7 pounds of body fat, which is a 12% reduction in body fat.

The case study with Derick Phan demonstrates Sprint 8 can improve physical performance, and significantly improve body composition by building muscle and reducing body fat.

Dr. Phan does Sprint 8 with the class on the Matrix Ascent Trainer (elliptical that elevates 10-seconds before the cardio sprint begins) with the *Sweat Score* measurement system. He also does Sprint 8 and practices sprinting and jumping technique on the S-Drive.

Derick Phan, age 45, doing triple jump workouts on turf and on the S-Drive. With two busy orthodontic practices, three small children at home, and coaching volleyball, his time is limited. But he is still competitive nationally.

*Derick Phan doing long-jump workouts on the S-Drive (above)
and speed training drive-phase starts on the S-Drive (below)*

Derick Phan doing rep #8 of Sprint 8 the way it's supposed to be done, all-out with everything you have for 30 seconds

Only 15 seconds to go showing on the Matrix Ascent Trainer control panel reverse-count down (left)

Hang on for 30 seconds

Life is good when Sprint 8 is done

14

E-Lift Technique

E-Lift technique discussed in my first book written in 1999, *Ready, Set, Go! Fitness* Chapters 9 and 10 describes a simple technique to recruit fast-muscle fiber so athletes and coaches work all three muscle-fiber types during strength training for superior results. This technique works best when used on push exercises where athletes are pushing resistance away from the center of the body.

To give credit where credit is due, the thinking behind the E-Lift technique comes from a long history of strength training. In a nutshell, the *slow and controlled negative* during the lowering phase of a bench press or a squat with the strategy of doing hard reps to a psyched-up failure (technically, momentary muscle fatigue) part of E-Lifts comes from Arthur Jones and my friend Dr. Ellington Darden.

Once the weight is in the lower position, the two second, *static-still pause* of E-Lift technique comes from the extremely strong Louie Simmons of West Side Barbell in Columbus, Ohio who coined the phrase *pause reps*.

The explosive, high-velocity, concentric push-the-bar-from-the-chest during a bench press or the *up-phase movement* during a squat without using momentum to start the movement, comes from my experience with sprinters doing reaction leg press to simulate track block starts. Once the weight is lowered and paused (athlete is still holding the weight), the coach or teammate says *SET* as if at the starting line, and claps hands simulating the starting gun while the athlete explodes from a no-momentum paused position.

The lowering phase in bench press and squats is technically the *eccentric movement*, and research in 2009 shows the eccentric movements during traditional strength training produces better results than *concentric* push movements.

Researchers report that the eccentric negative moment is important;

Meta-analyses showed that when eccentric exercise was performed at higher intensities compared with concentric training, total strength and eccentric strength increased more significantly. However, compared with concentric training, strength gains after eccentric training appeared more specific in terms of velocity and mode of contraction. Eccentric training performed at high intensities was shown to be more effective in promoting increases in muscle mass measured as muscle girth, (Roig, Marc & O'Brien, Kelly & Kirk, G & Murray, R & McKinnon, P & Shadgan, Babak & Reid, W Darlene. (2008). *The effects of eccentric versus concentric resistance training on muscle strength and mass in healthy adults: A systematic review with meta-analysis. British Journal of sports medicine 43. 556-68).*

Later in 2017, a major study shows the conclusion about the two parts of strength movements; concentric (push) vs. the eccentric (negative, bar lowering on bench press and squats) is not totally clear. Researchers report:

Although, ECC (eccentric) has been usually associated to greater increases in muscle mass compared to CON (concentric push) the present review clearly illustrated that the findings presented in the literature are too varied to clearly affirm which training mode leads to greater long-term muscle growth. Furthermore, **when both exercises paradigms are matched for either maximum load or work, the hypertrophic responses are very similar,** *(Franchi, MV. (2017) Skeletal Muscle Remodeling in Response to Eccentric vs. Concentric Loading: Morphological, Molecular, and Metabolic Adaptations. Front Physiol. 8: 447. Jul 4. doi: 10.3389/fphys.2017.00447. PMID: 28725197).*

Both movements are important, and E-Lift technique covers both the eccentric and the concentric movements during strength training exercises especially when there is a concentric pushing movement.

When someone does a traditional tempo of up on 2, down on 3 or 4, the *exercise paradox* is working to try not to recruit fast-muscle fiber. Only working slow-muscle fiber during strength training means that in order to get progressive overload for continued results, athletes will have to keep going longer and longer and heavier and heavier. Also, they may be only working slow-muscle fiber.

E-Lift technique shows you how to use *velocity of movement* to force the brain to recruit all three muscle-fiber types to propel the push movement so athletes get better results for sport applications.

E-Lift technique works extremely well during push exercises. Some call this a pause rep set, which is a cousin of E-Lift, but not the same. Pause reps emphasize the pause (and you do want to pause in a static-still position for two seconds), but pause reps don't emphasize the mission-critical aspect of the E-Lift technique -- the explosive, without momentum, fast-as-you-can, velocity push away-from-the-body, max-effort repetition during every rep of the set.

It looks like a pause rep, but it's significantly more intense because you are recruiting a lot more muscle fiber to propel the movement. For example, people who can do 100 push-ups will typically only be able to do 19 to 25 E-Lift technique push-ups before failing. Don't believe me? Put it to the test right now. If you don't pause, don't count the rep.

You have to fully stop and embellish the static-still pause in the lower position. Now, without momentum, explode up fast as possible as this simulates pushing movements in sports. Don't just drop down into the paused position. Control the movement as you lower your body down slow and controlled to the lower position and stop in a static-still position before the next explosive rep.

If you try this personally, you may notice (as many people do) that your brain takes over and it doesn't let you stop and pause on some reps. This is your brain trying to go back to slow fiber propelling the exercise and the *exercise paradox* won on those no-pause reps. Don't count the non-stop reps. Only count the reps where you come to a complete stop, pause, and without momentum, explode up fast-as-you-can. This is E-Lift technique.

You may also find yourself sweating on a push up or a chest press where you have never sweated before. This is because your heart muscle and lungs are having to work harder to oxygenate a lot more muscle fiber than before.

E-Lift technique is not necessarily opposite of the slow reps strength training strategy. Here's why. When performing a slow rep or a super-slow rep, you are increasing intensity by slowing down the velocity of movement. This can be positive for athletes in rehab because it creates micro-trauma in the muscles being worked while using less weight.

During strength training, athletes get intensity from the amount of resistance, number of sets & reps, and the *velocity of the movement*. While *slow reps* can be positive for some applications, the slow tempo does increase intensity with less weight and great for rehab, prehab, new-comers, and older adults. However, slow reps do not recruit fast-muscle fiber.

Thinking that slow reps recruit all three fiber types is the same thinking that sprinters need to jog longer and slower to get faster. Muscle recruitment doesn't work like this. The body adapts to the way it's trained -- train fast to be fast.

A great performance coach in Fair Hope, Alabama who has three decades of experience, Vince McConnell (*McConnellAthletics.com*) created a position-specific (DB and OLB) version of deadlifts used with E-Lift technique that I call *McConnell Deadlifts.* Terrance Timmons, former University of South Alabama team captain demonstrates *McConnell deadlifts* below with a position-specific, defensive back staggered stance using a Hex Bar.

Terrance Timmons in a DB staggered stance for McConnell Deadlifts. After a controlled down movement and two-second pause with weight slightly off the floor, he explodes up with E-Lift Technique

Another version of *McConnell Deadlifts* can be done in a Landmine format in the defensive back feet side-by-side starting position (below) with the weight slightly off the floor and paused before the explosive up movement.

From the static-still starting position, Terrance explodes up with max velocity without adding a slight momentum dip. This forces the recruitment all of three muscle-fiber types to get his fast fiber stronger and prepare his brain and nervous system for a common, full speed, position-specific movement.

Fast-Fiber Leg Workout

This is my favorite fast fiber leg workout. I know there are many ways to accomplish strength training for legs. And I am not saying this method is the best way. It is the best way I've found to get the job done in the shortest amount of time. There are three sets of a five-exercise superset. Training groups of six athletes don't have to wait on stations.

1. **Squats** or **McConnell Deadlifts** or **Leg Press**
   3X8-10 reps with E-lift technique

2. **Three-Way Calf Raises** 3X10-20
   #1 set - *Feet are toes-out, duck-footed*
   #2 set - *Feet are heels out, toes in pigeon-toed position*
   #3 set - *Feet are straight*

3. **Squat Jumps:** *High as possible every jump with a soft quiet landing as this insures plantars are being worked. Loud flat-footed landings mean the skeleton is getting the stress rather than leg muscles*
   #1 set - Wide-stance sumo jumps: *2.5-3 feet wide every jump, 8 reps*
   #2 set - Elongated lunge jumps: *5 reps each leg*
   Note: Jump elongated and land elongated
   #3 set - *Feet side-by-side. E-Lift technique, land soft in any position*

4. **Balance 10 seconds / 10 seconds** *Bosu balance 10 seconds (self-counted) on each foot. At the end of 10 seconds, athletes reach down and touch toes with opposite hand and fight for recovery before switching legs*

5. **Leg Curl** 3X10 *ankles plantar flexed first 5 reps dorsiflexed last 5 reps, this is the last set of the legs superset*

6. **Reverse Calf Raises** *1X failure - described in Train the Base (p.214)*

7. **Lockette Lunges** *3X8 each leg*

Lockette Lunges are named after the Seattle Seahawks WR Ricardo Lockette who did these lunge jumps preparing for the NFL Combines where he timed as one of the fastest receivers. *Lockette Lunges* are single-leg lunge jumps with a high knee during the jump and dorsiflexed ankle at the top of the jump. The rear foot stays on an elevated box for 3 sets of 8 reps per leg. Important point: The landing area needs to be padded.

Lockette Lunges demonstrated by coach Ryan Cali with 15-pound DBs. Notice the height of the single-leg lunge jump and the dorsiflexed ankle at the top of the jump. It's advisable to begin with body weight and progressively add resistance starting with one 5-pound plate held in the center of the body

Ricardo Lockette won the NCAA Division II 200m in 20.63. He clocked 100m in 10.28, and he was one of the fastest receivers in the 2011 NFL Combines

213

Train the Base with Reverse Calf Raises

For most of us, we live life on concrete. As human beings, we adapt by spending $21 *billion* a year on cushioned shoes with slightly elevated heels so our backs don't hurt when pounding the payment. We need these shoes. But at the same time, there is a downside for cushioned shoes.

Wearing these wonderfully cushioned shoes makes our feet weak and the achilles tendon and the biceps femoris (in the hamstrings muscle group) abnormally tight. I'm not saying to throw out your comfortable shoes. I am saying, however, it is wise to add a quick-and-easy exercise to strengthen the feet of your athletes.

Leg Presses not only work your quads, glutes and hamstrings, but you should notice that the bottom-of-your-feet burn like crazy during the last few reps. This means that you have recruited your plantar tendons, and they are being worked during this exercise to the point they are burning. This is positive.

When plantar tendons burn, this means they are creating micro-trauma in the plantar tendons. When the athletes sleep, their plantars heal back stronger. Plantars play an important role in achieving maximum stride length.

Reverse calf raises will work the tibialis (shin-splint muscles), and this exercise will also work the ligaments in the top of the feet. Reverse calf raises are simple to do.

Balancing with *arms holding on for balance in the rear*, stand on a step with body weight on the heels and mid-foot and toes hanging off the step as shown below by coach Tony DeMuro. While keeping the knees locked and straight, lower and raise toes as far as possible at a good pace.

To make this exercise effective, athletes need to bend at the hips where the upper and lower body are straight and bent in the middle with hips back. Hips back changes the angle and makes the exercise much more effective.

Pay close attention that the knees stay straight and locked and only your ankles are moving for a full range of motion up-and-down.

Only have the ankles working where toes are traveling up-and-down at a moderate pace until they slow down to near stop. One set to failure, once a week should add extra strength quickly. Don't stop the reps because the tibialis muscles are burning like crazy. The burning is a built-in barometer telling us the exercise is productive. The burn is training success.

At the same time athletes are working the tibialis, they are also working the ligaments in the top of the feet. Since these are ligaments, they don't have receptors for lactate like muscles do and athletes won't feel much of a burn in their feet, but they are being worked.

Reverse Calf Raises

Here's the test to know if this exercise is being done correctly. After one set to failure, walking immediately afterwards will feel strange. It will feel like the feet aren't connected to the body for a few minutes. Don't worry, the feeling will come back in a few minutes.

I recommend doing one set to failure once-a-week. If an athlete can't do 20 reps, he or she needs to do this exercise every other day for two weeks to catch up tibialis strength.

Hudson Walker, DE OLB, 6'5' 220 lbs. Soph
Redwood High School, Visalia California working on
speed technique before summer camps

15

Sprinting Athletes Need More Protein

When adding speed technique training and practicing full speed applying optimal technique three days a week, the body changes and it needs quality sleep and more protein. Research shows high-intensity sprinting athletes need more protein than endurance athletes.

The Institute of Medicine recommends adult women consume at least 46 grams of protein per day, and men need 56 grams each day. Sprinting athletes need more. They need more protein to help repair their muscles because they use all three muscle-fiber types during training.

People who do endurance types of exercise need more protein than those who do not exercise. Athletes who do speed training need more protein than those who do endurance training because the body is making a lot more positive hormones like growth hormone, testosterone and dopamine, (Coleman, Erin. (2018). *How Much Protein Per Day for Sprinters? Healthy Eating Dec 17.* | SF Gate, http://healthyeating.sfgate.com/much-protein-per-day-sprinters-6089.html).

Researchers report:

The current recommended intakes of protein for strength and endurance athletes are 1.6 to 1.7 grams per kilogram (of body weight) and 1.2 to 1.4 g/kg per day, respectively, (Fielding RA. (2002, Jul-Aug). *What are the dietary protein requirements of physically active individuals*, Nutr Clin Care).

Sprinting Increases Daily Protein Requirement

Endurance training athletes need 1 gram of protein X *50% of body weight per day* (1.2 to 1.4 grams per *kilogram* of body weight a day).

Sprinting sports athletes need 1 gram of protein X 75% *of body weight per day (*1.6 to 1.8 grams per kilogram body weight a day).

A quick-and-easy way to estimate the daily amount of protein when speed training is *one gram of protein per pound of body weight per day minus 20%.* Researchers report in a 2018 study:

> *There is robust evidence which shows that consuming protein pre- and/or post-workout induces a significant rise in muscle protein synthesis. It should be noted, however, that **total daily caloric and protein intake over the long term play the most crucial dietary roles in facilitating adaptations to exercise.** However, once these factors are accounted for, it appears that peri-exercise **protein intake, particularly in the post-training period, plays a potentially useful role in terms of optimizing physical performance and positively influencing the subsequent recovery processes for both resistance training and endurance exercise**,* (Cintineo, H. (2018). *Effects of Protein Supplementation on Performance and Recovery in Resistance and Endurance Training.* Front Nutr. 2018; 5: 83. Published online 2018 Sep 11. doi: 10.3389/fnut.2018.00083. PMCID: PMC6142015. PMID: 30255023)

It is wise to add more protein to the diet when doing intense speed training on a regular basis. Typically, high school and younger athletes end up being around 20 to 30 grams short of the protein they need daily to repair all three muscle-fiber types used in sprinting sports.

If you look closely, many of these athletes are missing 20 to 30 grams of protein from breakfast. Real food is always better than supplements, but for athletes who just can't stomach breakfast in the mornings, it's wise to find a protein supplement they can drink before school.

The *Academy of Nutrition and Dietetics, Dietitians of Canada,* and the *American College of Sports Medicine* published comprehensive guidelines on sports nutrition that shows 20 to 30 grams of protein during and after training is very positive for athletes:

> *Ingesting protein (approximately **20 grams to 30 grams** total protein, during exercise or the recovery period (post-exercise) **led to increased whole body and muscle protein synthesis** as well as improved nitrogen balance,* (Position Paper Nutrition and Athletic Performance, (2016, Feb). p 6. *www.dietitians.ca/sports*).

Gaining weight

While the purpose of this book is not athletic nutrition, I'll offer some practical tips I've seen work over the years to help athletes gain weight.

Frequently, what happens is athletes get home from practice partially dehydrated. They drink a glass or two of fluid and get full very quickly at the dinner table with a few bites because the stomach is full of fluid.

Here's the advice -- don't drink a lot before meals. Eat all the real food possible during dinner and push the protein down first, not the salad. The priority for sprinting-sport athletes needs to be the protein first because the salad may fill them up and suppress the hunger hormone ghrelin, which can make food nauseous to some athletes.

Here is a tip on how to gain weight. Once athletes are totally full of real food and just can't hold any more, go to the kitchen and pour a full glass of real chocolate milk, and kill it.

This simple plan has worked better for athletes to gain weight over the years than anything I've come across.

Now coach, if you want to lose weight, do two things. Three days a week, do the safe-on-the-hamstrings version of speed training -- Sprint 8 Cardio Protocol on a cardio machine. And when you get home, implement the gain weight plan in reverse. Drink all the water you can before meals. I know this is a simple plan, but it works.

Learning speed technique application from Ray Lewis (above) in how to read guards so I can help linebackers by eliminating the false-read step and going to where the ball is in the least number of steps. *Guards never lie*, says Ray.

What an honor to learn from the GOAT middle linebacker who was drafted in the first round and played all 17 years for the Baltimore Ravens. Ray was selected for the Pro Bowl 13 times and 10-times All-Pro. He won the NFL Defensive Player of the Year and led the Ravens to a record-setting defensive victory in Super Bowl XXXV where he received the Super Bowl MVP Award.

The stat that speaks to Ray's work ethic over the years is the fact he is one of only a few players in NFL history to play in a Pro Bowl in three different decades (1990s, 2000s, and 2010s). This doesn't happen without hours and hours of hard work preparing the body for one of the most physically demanding jobs on the planet, NFL middle linebacker.

.

16

Conclusion
"Greatness is Boring"

Talking with and learning from Ray Lewis while taking his three sons through two days of speed technique training, we discussed work ethic and the hours he spent training and studying film. He made a great statement that sums up what sports performance is all about.

He said, *greatness is boring.*

Those three words speak volumes. Greatness in sports, or anything worthwhile, may be perceived as boring by others. The great ones like Ray Lewis, Payton Manning, Wayne Gretzky are all known for their work ethic and putting in the hours of boring work to become great at their craft.

I remember Payton Manning being interviewed after his brother Eli was drafted. *What did you tell Eli to help him get ready for the transition from college to the pros,* asked the reporter? Payton replied, *I just told him this is the NFL. And that is Ray Lewis over there.*

I think this was Payton's nice way of saying, this is a huge step up in speed and intensity and you better be ready to work hard because the guy on the other side outworks everyone. This athlete watches film for hours and learns every little thing about you and the offensive line that protects you. And he trains hard and will have his body and mind in supreme condition to go hard on every play.

How can a guy start 17 years in the NFL as a middle linebacker and be extremely successful year after year? All Pro 13 years, two Super Bowl wins, and a Super bowl MVP selection. This is near unbelievable success! But Ray Lewis did the boring work and put in the hours. His boring work paid off.

Middle linebacker in the NFL isn't an easy job. There are two guards, two tackles and a tight end or two on the other side, and one of them, sometimes two, have the assignment to knock your head off and keep you from doing your job. But Ray Lewis did the work because he realized early in life it had to be done.

He wore #52 because he used 52 playing cards for a daily workout during high school to help get him to the NFL. He would pick one of 52 cards. If the card was a 7, he did 7 push-ups. He would flip the next card for the number for the next set of push-ups. He went through the entire deck for his push-up workout with jacks, queens, and kings counting 10, aces 25 and jokers 50. Once finished, he would use a second deck for sit-ups.

If speed technique training had a theme song, it would be *greatness is boring.* Sprinting full-speed reps is hard work. There is nothing more intense on the human body if it's done correctly. With speed training, effort at 95% doesn't count.

To get faster, athletes must do a full-speed workout with optimal technique three days a week and perform a set of very specific movements for linear, lateral and functional speed. *Functional speed* meaning practicing the exact movements for their positions full-speed fast with optimal technique.

As we have seen throughout this book, many athletes in almost all sprinting sports try to sprint too tall and upright. They succumb to the *exercise paradox* of the body trying to propel human movement with slow-muscle fiber in the endurance energy system because it's easy.

Most athletes don't know optimal speed technique of how to position the body to propel the movement of sprinting with the strongest and fastest muscle fiber in the body, which just happens to be the hardest way for the human body to move. The heart muscle and lungs have to work at their top limit to oxygenate quite literally twice the muscle fiber as when running at less than full speed.

When untrained athletes sprint, they generally remain too tall and upright and move their legs and arms as fast as possible. This is how most athletes and runners position their bodies naturally, until they become speed technique trained.

Coach, you have the tools to teach optimal speed technique in two sessions. This should perhaps be the starting point for all strength & conditioning training.

Learning to apply optimal speed technique for *position-specific functional movements* can take a lot of time performing reps at 100%, all-out, full-speed intensity with supreme mental focus to reprogram the brain to move faster, or it simply doesn't count.

Success in sports performance training generally comes down to getting an athlete to where he or she is going faster. For strength & conditioning coaches, you can present the head coach with data showing your athletes should be getting faster because they are much stronger on paper, but when the dust settles, team performance improvement comes when the whole team is getting to where they are going faster.

While there are many different ways to look at sports performance, ultimately team speed has to be at the top of the list.

Once the team has speed technique somewhat mastered in two sessions focused exclusively on linear and lateral speed technique, the goal then becomes practicing with optimal speed technique for functional, position-specific movements. This only happens when practicing at 100% speed intensity for a minimum of 8 reps three days a week so the fast fiber propelling athletic movements get recruited and traumatized. Now, athletes will keep getting stronger and stronger as the three muscle-fiber types heal during sleep.

In conclusion, it has been an honor to produce this book to help you coach athletes in sprinting sports like football, baseball, softball, soccer, rugby, lacrosse, and track & field in the mechanics optimal speed technique with a system of training that will help your athletes get where they are going faster.

Whether you are a head coach, assistant coach, professional strength & conditioning coach, or coach mom or coach dad, I hope you have received information to help you help your athletes live up to their potential.

Please consider emailing a report of how speed technique training has worked for your athletes, your team, or your children, and I will share it with others as motivation. My email is phil7@40speed.com

Have a great day!

The speed technique camp finished. Time to celebrate!

Ray Lewis III, coach Doug Lawson, Rian Finney and dad, LaRian Finney, NFL Hall of Fame & Super Bowl MVP Ray Lewis, Rahsaan Lewis, Phil Campbell and Ralin Lewis at the Under Armour Global HQ Performance Center powered by Fitness FX in Baltimore

References

Ahmaidi, (1998). "Effects of interval training at ventilatory thresholds on clinical and cardiorespiratory responses in elderly humans." Eur J Appl Physiol Occup Physiol. Jul;78(2):170-6.).

Bayat, A. (2011). "Practical model of low-volume high-intensity interval training induces performance and metabolic adaptations that resemble 'all-out' sprint interval training." Sports Sci Med. 2011 Sep 1;10(3):571-6. 2011).

Benoit, laborde. (2016). "The Quest for the Perfect Athlete." DVD L'Harmattan, The French Connection. Arte France.

Boecker H, (2008). "The runner's high: opioidergic mechanisms in the human brain. Cerebral cortex" (New York, N.Y. : 1991), 18 (11), 2523-31 PMID: 18296435)

Borst, (2001). "Effects of resistance training on insulin-like growth factor-1 and IGF binding proteins." Med Sci Sports Exerc. Apr;33(4):648-653).

Burgomaster KA,,Gibala MJ., (2005). Si x sessions of sprint interval training increases muscle capacity in humans. 2005, J Appl Physiol.

Burt, D. (2012)."Targeting exercise-induced growth hormone release: A novel approach to fighting obesity by substantially increasing endogenous GH serum levels naturally."KDMC, Brookhaven, MS, http://www.readysetgofitness.com/obesity_research2. shtml.

Chwalbinski-Moneta. (1996). "Threshold increases in plasma growth hormone in relation to plasma catecholamine and blood lactate concentration during progressive exercise in endurance-trained athletes." Eur J Appl Physiol Occup Physiol. 73(1-2):117-20).
Colgan, Michael. (1993). Optimum Sports Nutrition, Your Competitive Edge. New York, NY. Advanced Research Press.

DiNicolantonio, J. (2017), "The Salt Fix: Why the Experts Got It All Wrong-and How Eating More Might Save Your Life." Harmony Books, New York.

Dintiman, G. Ward, B. Tellez, T. (1997) "Sports Speed, Second Edition." Human Kinetics, Champaign IL

Duchateau J, (2014) "Maximal discharge rate of motor units determines the maximal rate of force development during ballistic contractions in human." Front Hum Neurosci. 2014 Apr 22;8:234. https://www.ncbi.nlm.nih.gov/pmc/articles/PMC4001023/

Dudley G (1982). "Influence of exercise intensity and duration on biochemical adaptations in skeletal muscle." J. Appl. Phsiol, 53, 844-850).

Farhead N, Punt TD. Silencing Sharapova's grunt improves the perception of her serve speed. Perceptual and motor skills. 2015 Jun;120(3):722–30. pmid:26057416

Fung, J, DiNicolantonio, J. (2019). "The Longevity Solution: Rediscovering Centuries-Old Secrets to a Healthy, Long Life," (pp 148-163) Victory Belt Pub, Las Vegas.

Gastin, PB. (2001). "Energy system interaction and relative contribution during maximal exercise." Sports Med 2001;31(10):725-41. PMID: 115478894.

Gibala. (2000),"Nutritional supplementation and resistance exercise: what is the evidence for enhanced skeletal muscle hypertrophy?" Can J Appl Physiol. Dec;25(6):524).

Gilbala, M. Burgomaster K, (2005). "Six sessions of sprint interval training increases muscle oxidative potential and cycle endurance capacity in humans."J Appl Physiol. Jun.

Gist N. (2014) "Sprint interval training effects on aerobic capacity: a systematic review and meta-analysis. Sports Med. 2014 Feb;44(2):269-79).

Godfrey, RJ. (2003) "The exercise-induced growth hormone response in athletes." Sports Medicine. 33(8):599-613).

Godfrey RJ, (2009). "The role of lactate in the exercise-induced human growth hormone response: evidence from McArdle disease." Br J Sports Med. 2009 Jul;43(7).

Gordon, Kraemer, Vos, Lynch, Knuttgen. (1994). "Effect of acid-base on growth hormone response to acute high-intensity cycle exercise." J Appl Physiol. Feb;76(2):821).

Holloszy, J. (1967). "Effects of Exercise on Mitochondrial Oxygen Uptake and Respiratory Enzyme Activity in Skeletal Muscle," J of Biological Chemistry, vol. 242(9), pp. 2278-2282.

Ikai M, Steinhaus AH. Some factors modifying the expression of human strength. Journal of Applied Physiology. 1961 Jan 1;16(1):157–63.

Jenkins. (1999). "Growth hormone and exercise." Clin Endocrinol (Oxf). Jun;50(6):683-9. PMID: 10468938.

Jesper, Anderson, Schjerling, Saltin. (2000). Muscles, Genes and Athletic Performance." Scientific American. Sept(1)48-55.

Kastello, Sothmann, Murthy. (1993). "Young and old subjects for aerobic capacity have similar noradrenergic responses to exercise." J Appl Physiol. Jan;74(1):49-54).

Know, Lee (2018). "Mitochondria and the Future of Medicine." Chelsea Green Piblishing, White River, Vermont.

Krzywkowski, (2001). "Effects of glutamine supplementation on exercise-induced changes in lymphocyte function." Am J Physiol Cell Physiol. Oct;281(4):C1259-65).

Linden, D. (2012). "Exercise, pleasure and the brain Understanding the biology of "runner's high," Psychology Today, Apr 21.

Llorens-Martin, (2009) *Mechanisms mediating brain plasticity: IGF1 and adult hippocampal neurogenesis. The Neuroscientist,* 15, 134-148).

Marcinik (1991.) "Effects of strength training on lactate thresholds and endurance performance." Med Sci Sports Ex. Jun;23(6):739-43.

Medbo, Burgers. (1990). "Effect of training on the anaerobic capacity." Med Sci Sports Exerc. Aug;22(4):501-7. PMID: 2402211.

Medbo, Tabata. (1989). "Relative importance of aerobic and anaerobic energy release during short-lasting exhausting bicycle exercise." J Appl Physiol. Nov;67(5):1881.

Meirleir,(1986). "Beta-endorphin and ACTH levels in peripheral blood during and after aerobic and anaerobic exercise." Eur J Appl Physiol Occup Physiol. 55(1):5-8).

Mirkin, G. (2016). "How to Strengthen Your Heart," www.DrMirkin.com, http://drmirkin.com/public/ezine080705.html. "Collapse After Exercise."http://drmirkin.com/fitness/collapse.html

Mujika, Chatard, Busso, Geyssant, Barale, Lacoste. (1995). "Effects of training on performance in competitive swimming." Can J Appl Physiol. Dec;20(4):395-406).

Mujika, Padilla, Ibanez, Izquierdo, Gorostiaga. (2000). "Creatine supplementation and sprint performance in soccer." Med Sci Sports Exerc. Feb;32(2):518-25).

Nalcakan GR. (2014). "The Effects of Sprint Interval vs. Continuous Endurance Training on Physiological And Metabolic Adaptations in Young Healthy Adults." J Hum Kinet. 2014 Dec 30;44:97-109.

Nevill M, (1996). "Growth hormone responses to treadmill sprinting in sprint- and endurance trained athletes." Eur J Appl Occup Physiol. 72(5-6):460-7).

O'Connell DG, Hinman MR, Hearne KF, Michael ZS, Nixon SL. The effects of "grunting" on serve and forehand „h„, in collegiate tennis players. The Journal of Strength & Conditioning Research. 2014 Dec 1;28(12):3469–75.

O'Connell DG, Brewer JF, Man TH, Weldon JS, Hinman MR. The Effects of Forced Exhalation and Inhalation, Grunting, and Valsalva Maneuver on Forehand Force in Collegiate Tennis Players. The Journal of Strength & Conditioning Research. 2016 Feb 1;30(2):430–7.

Oliver TD. (2015) "Endurance vs. interval sprint training and/or resistance training; impact on microvascular dysfunction in type 2 diabetes." Am J Physiol Heart Circ Physiol. 2015 Sep 25:ajpheart.00440.2015).

Pritzlaff, Wideman, Weltman, J., Abbott, Gutgesell, Hartman, Veldhuis, Weltman, A. (2000). "Catecholamine release, growth hormone secretion, and energy expenditure during exercise vs. recovery in men." J Appl Physiol. Sept;89(3):937-46.

Pritzlaff, Wideman, Weltman, J., Abbott, Gutgesell, Hartman, Veldhuis, Weltman, A. (2000). "Impact of acute exercise intensity on pulsatile growth hormone release in men." J Appl Physiol. Aug;87(2):498-504. PMID: 10444604.

Ratey, J. (2008). "SPARK, The New Revolutionary New Science of Exercise and the Brain." (Little Brown and Company.

Roberts, Wilson. (1999). "Effect of stretching duration on active and passiverange of motion in the lower extremity." Br J Sports Med. Aug;33(4):259-63. PMID: 10450481.

Ronsen, Haug, Pedersen, Bahr. (2001). "Increased neuroendocrine response to a repeated bout of endurance exercise." Med Sci Sports Exerc. Apr;33(4):568-75).

Schilling. (2001). "Creatine supplementation and health variables: a retrospective study." Med Sci Sports Exerc. Feb;33(2):183-8. PMID: 11224803.

Sinnett S, Kingstone A. A preliminary investigation regarding the effect of tennis grunting: does white noise during a tennis shot have a negative impact on shot perception?. PloS one. 2010 Oct 1;5(10):e13148. pmid:20957210

Stokes (2002). "Growth Hormone responses to repeated maximal cycle ergometer exercise at different pedaling rates." J Appl Physiol 2992 Feb;92(2):602-8).

Stone, (1999). "Effects of in-season (5-weeks) creatine and pyruvate supplements on anaerobic performance and body composition in American football players." Int J Sport Nutr. Jun;9(2):146-65).

Suminski, (1997) "Acute effect of amino acid ingestion and resistance exercise on plasma growthhormone concentration in young men." Int Journal Sports Nutrition, March;7(1):48-60).

Tabrizi, McIntryre, Quesnel, Howard. (2000). "Limited dorsiflexion predisposes to injuries of the ankle in children." J Bone Joint Surg Br. Nov;82(8):1103-6).

Taylor, Bachman. (1999). "The effects of endurance training on muscle-fiber types and enzyme activities." Can J Appl Physiol. Feb;24(1):41-53. PMID: 9916180.

Trappe, Costill, Thomas. (2000). "Effect of swim taper on whole muscle and single muscle fiber contractile properties." Med Sci Sports Exerc.Dec;32(12):48-56).

VanHelder, Goode, Radomski. (1984). "Effects of anaerobic and aerobic exercise of equal duration and work expenditure on plasma growth hormone levels."Eur J Appl Physiol Occup Physiol. 52(3):255-7. PMID: 6539675.

Vanhelder, (1985). "Hormonal and metabolic response to three types of exercise of equal duration and external work output."Eur J Appl Occup Physiol. 54(4):337-42).

Vanhelder, Radomski, Goode. (1984). "Growth hormone responses during intermittent weight lifting exercise in Men." Eur J Physiol Occup Physiol. 53(1):31-4).

Vincent G. (2015). "Changes in mitochondrial function and mitochondria associated protein expression in response to 2-weeks of high intensity interval training." Front Physiol. Feb 24;6:51).

Wahl P, (2013). "Effects of active vs. passive recovery during Wingate-based training on the acute hormonal, metabolic and psychological response." Growth Horm IGF Res. 2013 Dec;23(6):201-8).

Welbourne, TC. (2002). "Boost Your Growth Hormone Output Through Amino Acid Supplements," Dept. of Molecular Cellular Physiology, LSU Medical Center.

Welbourne, TC. (1995). "Increased plasma bicarbonate and growth hormoneafter an oral glutamine load." American Journal of Clinical Nutrition, Vol.61,1058-1061. National Library of Science, PubMed abstract: 7733028.

Welch AS, Tschampl M. Something to shout about: a simple, quick performance enhancement technique improved strength in both experts and novices. Journal of Applied Sport Psychology. 2012 Oct 1;24(4):418–28.

Weltman, Pritzlaff, Wideman, Blumer, Abbott, Hartman, Veldhuis. (2000). "Exercise-dependent growth hormone release is linked to markers of heightened central adrenergic outflow." J Appl Physiol. Aug;89(2):629-35.

Weltman, Weltman, Womack, Davis, Blumer, Gasser, Hartman. (1997). "Exercise training decreases the growth hormone (GH) response to acute constant-load exercise." Med Sci Sports Exer. May;29(5):660-76.
Widrick, (1996.) "Force-velocity and force- Power properties of single fiber from elite master runners and sedentary med." Am J Physiol. Aug;271 (2Pt 1):C676-83.

Whyte LJ, (2010). "Effect of 2 weeks of sprint interval training on health-related outcomes in sedentary overweight/obese men." Metabolism. Oct;59(10):1421-8.).

Woynarowski, D. Fossel, M. Blackurn, G, (2011). "The Immortality Edge." (Wiley p.86-7) Hoboken, New Jersey.

Index

About the Author

Phil Campbell, M.S., M.A., ACSM-CPT, FACHE-R

Phil Campbell has a lifetime of experience in researching best practices and creating new and innovative ways to achieve award-winning levels of performance. He has coached over 20,000 athletes over the years.

As a Speed Technique Coach, athletes attending his two-day camps have achieved superior levels of performance. Athletes like New England Patriots Super Bowl MVP Julian Edelman and Seattle Seahawks Ricardo Lockette, who was one of the fastest receivers in the NFL Combines and retired with several Super Bowl rings, have been to Phil Campbell for speed technique training.

Super Bowl MVP Ray Lewis and Jerry Rice, three time Super Bowl winner, have trusted Phil Campbell to teach speed technique to their sons. Raymond Berry, who was the Jerry Rice of his day, recommends Phil's teachings.

He has been a university strength & conditioning coach and track coach. Currently, athletes from across the U.S. and Canada travel to him for his two-session speed technique training camps.

Phil Campbell's undergraduate degree is from Middle Tennessee State University, and he holds two advanced degrees; M.S. from Central Michigan University and M.A. from Liberty University. He is professionally certified by the American College of Sports Medicine ACSM C-PT and the American College of Healthcare Executives, FACHE-R.

Due to numerous requests from coaches to learn his speed technique teaching methods, he created a specialty certification for Speed Technique and this book serves as the textbook.

As a 6'2" 225 pound USAT&F Masters 100 and 200 meter sprinter, discus and javelin thrower, he understands exactly how to train athletes of all sizes and elite athletes to run much faster.

He is the creator of the Sprint 8 Cardio Protocol that is featured in award-winning cardio units made by Matrix Fitness for over 15 years. He is the author of *Ready, Set, Go! Fitness*, a 384-page fitness book with 170-research citations. Initially published in 2000, this book is now in the second edition, ninth printing. He authored the *Sprint 8 Cardio Protocol* in 2016 after conducting two hospital-based research projects investigating the impact of the Sprint 8 Protocol on exercise-induced growth hormone, cholesterol reduction, sprint-intensity cardio vs. statin drugs, and body composition.

Phil Campbell has been cited as an expert in exercise-induced growth hormone, anaerobic exercise and speed technique. He teaches a three-hour CEU/CEC approved course across the US that certifies coaches and trainers to teach the Sprint 8 Cardio Protocol. He is originally from Tennessee and now based in San Jose, California.

Find a Speed Technique Coach in your area
who has been through Phil Campbell's Speed Technique
Coach Specialization course visit

www.40speed.com

*Ray Lewis III perfecting speed technique at the
Under Armour Global HQ Performance Center
powered by FX Fitness in Baltimore, Maryland*

*Working with Jerry Rice Jr. on speed technique
at the Riekes Center in Menlo Park, California
www.Riekes.org*